kamera
B O O K S

www.kamerabooks.co.uk

Roland Thorne

SAMURAI FILMS

kamera
BOOKS

First published in 2008 by Kamera Books
P.O.Box 394, Harpenden, Herts, AL5 1XJ
www.kamerabooks.com

copyright © Roland Thorne, 2008
Series Editor: Hannah Patterson

The right of Roland Thorne to be identified as the author of this work has been
asserted in accordance with the Copyright, Designs and Patents Act 1988.

All rights reserved. No part of this book may be reproduced, stored
in or introduced into a retrieval system, or transmitted, in any form
or by any means (electronic, mechanical, photocopying, recording or
otherwise) without the written permission of the publishers.

Any person who does any unauthorised act in relation to this publication
may be liable to criminal prosecution and civil claims for damages.

A CIP catalogue record for this book is available from the British Library.

ISBN 13: 978-1-84243-255-6

2 4 6 8 10 9 7 5 3 1

Typeset by Avocet Typeset, Chilton, Aylesbury, Bucks
Printed by Dami Editorial & Printing Services Co Ltd, China

For Mum, Dad and Sal.

CENTRAL ARKANSAS LIBRARY SYSTEM
SIDNEY S. McMATH BRANCH LIBRARY
LITTLE ROCK, ARKANSAS

CONTENTS

ACKNOWLEDGEMENTS

Special thanks to Craig Cormick, for his vital help and encouragement during the early stages of this project. Thanks also to those who have taught me the most about film and writing: Dave Watson, Francesca Rendle-Short and Felicity Packard. Thanks to my good friend Chris 'Quaddy' Williams for his invaluable help with the frame grabs. Thanks to those who have already written on this fascinating subject, mainly Mitsuhiro Yoshimoto, Alain Silver and Patrick Galloway. Thanks to Eastern Eye for making so many of these wonderful films available in Australia. And, of course, a big thanks to Hannah Patterson, for seeing the potential of a Kamera Book on samurai films.

INTRODUCTION

Imagine a mountain top, with long grass undulating in the unrelenting wind. Two figures come into view, a few short paces away from each other. Their firm stance conveys pride, determination and a strange sort of calm. In a flurry of motion, one of the men draws his sword, quickly followed by the other. With a flash of blades, and a mist of blood, it is over. One man walks away, the other doesn't. Who are these men? How did they get to the point where violence was the only way to settle their dispute? And why did they both seem unafraid to die? Welcome to the world of the samurai film.

Samurai films come in many flavours: there are the basic action movies, beautiful in their brutal simplicity, the meaningful and moving tales of the individual's struggle to survive, and the expansive, epic films that tell tales of famous personalities. In short, there's something to please every fan of genre cinema. Within the pages of this book you'll find everything you need to begin or continue an interest in this highly entertaining and unique genre. There's basic information on the samurai and their world, details on the major directors and stars, and reviews of some of the finest films in the genre.

Every film reviewed here is easily available. This is a rule I've stuck to fervently while writing this book. It meant excluding some great films, such as Hideo Gosha's *Tenchu*, but if you can't easily see them I've decided not to extensively review them. There are few things I find more frustrating than buying a book about a genre, and discovering that most of the films reviewed have not been available for many years. At the time of writing, all but four of the films reviewed in this book are available on DVD from Amazon.com. These four films – *Three Outlaw Samurai*, *Bandits vs. Samurai Squadron*, *Hunter in the Dark* and *Samurai Saga* – can be purchased from importers, and are not at all hard to find.

So, happy viewing... Many excellent films await you.

A NOTE ON JAPANESE NAMES

In Japanese, it is the family name that comes first when an individual's name is included in any form of text. This is the opposite of the convention in English, where the family name comes second. For example, in English my name is written Roland Thorne, but in traditional Japanese I might be referred to as Thorne Roland. To avoid confusion for those with only a limited knowledge of the Japanese language (a category I certainly fall into) I have chosen to follow the English convention in this book. As you explore the samurai film genre, you will probably notice that some books, articles and sub-titles on some of the films follow the Japanese convention.

WHO WERE THE SAMURAI?

Put simply, the samurai were a warrior class, forming the armies of feudal leaders during Japan's many civil wars between the 10th and 15th centuries, and during the relatively peaceful Tokugawa period (1603-1868). They wore distinctive armour and fought with weapons and styles unique to Japan.

There are many aspects of the samurai's life which constantly crop up in samurai films, and these may confuse those unfamiliar with them. What follows is a summary of the main issues of samurai life, which are commonly referenced in the films, as well as a brief summary of the historical periods in which the films are usually set.

CULTURED WARRIORS

The importance of the samurai in Japan's early civil wars gradually led to them becoming an important social class, the more powerful samurai becoming daimyo, feudal lords ruling a clan, and the warriors and peasants beneath him. Many of these daimyo began to study the fine arts, in what has been described by many scholars as an attempt to legitimise their rule over the uneducated peasants. Most of these daimyo insisted their samurai do the same, so the samurai became a highly educated warrior class, not only skilled at warfare, but also at arts such as painting, sculpture, calligraphy, poetry, and traditional dance and theatre. This created in the samurai an interesting contradiction: a man who could write a beautiful haiku one day, and strike his enemy down the next. Of course, to the samurai, there was no contradiction; both poetry and swordsmanship were considered arts, and there was beauty to be found in both.

THE DAISHO

The daisho were the two swords carried by the samurai, usually a katana (long sword) and a wakazashi (short sword). In the Tokugawa period there was actually a law which stated only samurai were allowed to carry both a short and long blade. These swords were immensely important to the samurai; they symbolised his position in the warrior class, and were described by many as the very soul of the warrior. Even a samurai in the most desperate of situations would be loath to give up his swords.

BUSHIDO

Focused on honour and obedience, the code of bushido has done much to colour how we view the samurai, specifically giving rise to the myth of all samurai being morally outstanding individuals obsessed with honour. The underlying principles of the bushido code are loyalty and obedience; the ideal samurai puts the wishes of his daimyo and clan above his own, and is prepared to die for them. Also important to bushido is a sense of honour, something which was tied closely to each samurai's reputation.

However, the historical reality is far from the ideal. Any close examination of how the samurai conducted themselves in times of war reveals that the vast majority followed the bushido code only when it suited them. In truth, the samurai were much like many other warrior classes which have arisen throughout history. They strove to be the best at warfare they possibly could, and placed more importance on victory than on honour.

Both the mythical bushido samurai and his more brutal historical counterpart, have been the subject of many Japanese films. Regardless of his mythic status, the samurai always makes a compelling protagonist.

SEPPUKU AND HARA-KIRI

Part of the bushido code focused on ritual suicide, known as seppuku, or, more crudely, as hara-kiri. A samurai could be ordered by his daimyo to commit seppuku in punishment for some wrongdoing, or may have chosen to do so in the hope of absolving himself of some personal shame. Seppuku could also be used as a form of protest, a signed letter outlining the samurai's grievance. A death through seppuku was considered much more honourable than being killed by enemies, so if a battle was completely hopeless, a samurai might consider seppuku. The actual ritual involved making a long deep cut across the stomach. When this was done an assistant would complete the process by swiftly beheading the samurai, putting an end to his suffering.

RONIN

The term *ronin* literally means *wave man*, suggesting an individual adrift on the ocean, his future decided by the uncaring waves and currents. Ronin were masterless samurai, and there were many ways a samurai could end up unemployed. He may have displeased his daimyo, and been dismissed from his service. When daimyo were defeated in battle, and their lands taken by another, their samurai were usually left unemployed. It was also possible to be born a ronin. The strict class system of feudal Japan made it difficult for the ronin to fit into society; no longer able to fulfil the role he was born to, the ronin was also often too proud to give up his swords and become a farmer or merchant. Some lucky ronin were able to find employment with other daimyo. Others became bandits, or bodyguards and teachers to wealthy members of the lower classes. Many suffered dire poverty, unable to afford food and lodgings. The Tokugawa period produced many ronin. With the Tokugawa government regularly dissolving clans which displeased them, many samurai were left homeless and unemployed, forced to wander the roads.

Ronin in samurai films are typically portrayed as much more effective individuals than samurai in service. In many ways the two are polar opposites of each other: the employed samurai well dressed and cultured, the ronin unkempt and rude. However, the ronin's tougher lifestyle has often equipped him with a much more cunning and creative mind. A common plot in samurai films is that of a ronin using his abilities to help employed samurai overcome difficulties they aren't equipped to handle themselves (see *Sanjuro* and *Kill!*). The ronin, with his much freer lifestyle, is often used to show the shortcomings of the employed samurai's life of mindless obedience. Sometimes ronin characters are even used to illustrate the moral deficiencies in this code. The best examples of this are the films of Masaki Kobayashi, in which there is a stark contrast between compassionate ronin and uncaring samurai.

HISTORICAL CONTEXT

Most samurai films take place in either the Sengoku or Tokugawa periods of Japanese history. The Sengoku period (1478–1603) was a time of chaos for Japan; rival daimyo (lords in charge of a clan and an army) battled to control the nation, and these constant wars meant that nobody's safety was guaranteed. Samurai films set in this era often focus on actual historical events, as is the case with *Samurai Banners* and *Kagemusha*, and as a result tend to feature large-scale battles in all their splendour.

In stark contrast to this is the Tokugawa period (1603–1868). A daimyo named Ieyasu Tokugawa emerged from the Sengoku period victorious, and through various means was able to control the daimyo, preventing any challenges to his position as Shogun (military dictator in charge of Japan). This time of stability and peace became known as the Tokugawa period, and would last for the next 267 years, as Ieyasu's descendants continued his rule. Ieyasu's methods for maintaining peace in Japan involved establishing a regime of strict laws, with harsh penalties for disobedience. Japan's already stringent class system became law, and travel was restricted through the use of passes and carefully guarded checkpoints. The daimyo were kept in line through the very clever tactic of having them spend every second year in Edo (Ieyasu's new capital of Japan, later to become Tokyo), with their immediate families forced to live there permanently. This prevented the daimyo from planning elaborate campaigns or mustering troops in their territory, and the fact that the Tokugawa had easy access to their families ensured their obedience. Also, the Tokugawa showed no qualms about using their power to completely disband clans which failed to obey them, and this constant threat also served to ensure the loyalty of the daimyo.

The majority of samurai films are set in the Tokugawa period. Some involve clans that try to avoid destruction at the hands of the oppressive Tokugawa, and others present the Tokugawa in a more positive way, as brave men doing whatever it takes to preserve the peace. However, most of the films set in the Tokugawa period focus on the lives of individuals, in contrast to films set in the Sengoku period, which are often concerned with the epic histories of daimyo and their clans. One common theme is the plight of the samurai in a time of peace; what does one skilled at warfare do, when there are no wars? Many films set in the Tokugawa period describe the exploits of wandering ronin (masterless samurai), whose numbers were greatly increased during this time.

WHAT MAKES A SAMURAI FILM?

The term 'samurai film' is an invention of American film critics, and is rarely used in Japan. The Japanese prefer to group their films into two main genres, *jidaigeki* (which very roughly translates as 'period drama') and *gendaigeki* (films with a contemporary setting). Within these two genres are a huge selection of sub-genres, creating what is perhaps the most detailed cinema genre classification system in the world.

The *jidaigeki* films are often concerned with a very specific time in Japan's history, the Tokugawa era (1603-1868), which was a time of relative peace for Japan after centuries of civil war. As period dramas, it is unsurprising that many (but not all) *jidaigeki* are concerned with the samurai and other sword-wielding warriors of Tokugawa-era Japan. Indeed, *jidaigeki*, which are mainly concerned with swordplay, have their own sub-genre, *chambara* or 'sword drama'. Many of the films reviewed in this book could be correctly classified as *chambara*, but I cannot help but feel that this description doesn't do them justice. There is, after all, a lot more to these films than sword fights.

These considerations make the samurai film quite a difficult genre to define, and for the purposes of this book a definition separate to those such as *jidaigeki* and *chambara* is required. Forming such a definition may seem easy at first; surely samurai films are simply films concerned with the samurai? Unfortunately this definition is a bit *too* simple. It excludes a great many films generally assumed to be of the samurai genre, such as the *Zatoichi* and *Lady Snowblood* series, whose main protagonists are of peasant birth rather than the samurai class. Perhaps it is easier to find a common theme or motif among the films. Swordplay would seem to be a safe bet. Surely all samurai films include swordplay? Again, this is problematic. The true samurai film deals with more than just swordplay. Indeed, some samurai films contain very little action at all.

It is, more accurately, what goes on behind the swordplay that best defines the samurai film. More specifically, samurai films are concerned with the problems and dilemmas (both internal and external) of the warrior, of the one who is skilled at performing violent acts. The true samurai film forces its protagonist into situations where either they or the audience (or both) learn something new about the status of the individual as killer. Whether it's Kambei from *Seven Samurai* learning that he, and all other samurai, will eventually fade from history, or Sanjuro or Zatoichi, deciding that a life without killing would be better, but not knowing how to achieve that goal, the samurai film is concerned with the learning journey of the warrior.

Added to this is the iconography and setting of the samurai film. Pre-industrial Japan, usually the Tokugawa period (1603-1868), forms the setting. This allows for intrigue among the samurai in the larger cities and castles, or bloody battles between ronin (wandering masterless samurai) and yakuza (criminal gangs) in the smaller towns and villages. The iconography consists of a variety of things, but perhaps most important is the sword: the essential instrument of the warrior. The distinctive appearance of the Japanese sword or *katana* will forever be associated with the samurai film and, together with the pre-industrial Japanese setting and warrior's learning journey, goes a long way towards defining it.

OTHER RECURRING THEMES AND PLOT ELEMENTS

DEPICTIONS OF NATURE

Like many cultures, the Japanese have a rich tradition of the depiction of nature in their art. However, unlike most cultures, this tradition made the transition into the cinema, and is a dominant aspect of many Japanese films. As such, many samurai films contain long, beautiful scenes of the distinctive Japanese landscape, something most noticeable in the breathtaking work of Akira Kurosawa and Hiroshi Inagaki. As Patrick Galloway* has pointed out, these depictions of nature are often symbolic, and tap into an artistic language which is familiar to Japanese audiences, but not to international viewers. For example, falling cherry blossoms are often symbolic of the way death can strike suddenly and unexpectedly. These symbols are not crucial to enjoying the films, but, if understood, will enrich the viewer's experience. As such, a little research on Japanese artistic traditions can be immensely rewarding.

* Patrick Galloway's *Stray Dogs and Lone Wolves* is a detailed guide to samurai films, and highly recommended as further reading.

THE GIRI/NINJO CONFLICT

The word *ninjo* refers to the more emotional feelings of human beings, sentiments such as sympathy, love and the emotional decisions we make governing what is right and wrong. *Giri* means duty to your superiors. For the samurai, who was supposed to be unquestionably obedient, the giri/ninjo conflict is particularly important. What if he is ordered to do something which goes against his conscience, or threatens someone he has an emotional attachment to? He is supposed to obey without question, but this is much easier said than done… The giri/ninjo conflict is a constant theme in the samurai film, and one which makes for some very dramatic and compelling plots. I haven't included the giri/ninjo conflict as part of my definition of the genre, simply because it isn't present in all of the films; there are a great many samurai films where the protagonist is no longer (or never has been) governed by giri, thus preventing any conflict with their emotional impulses.

THE DIRECTORS

AKIRA KUROSAWA

The most internationally famous and acclaimed Japanese director, Akira Kurosawa is the master filmmaker responsible for some of the finest films ever made. He started his film career for Toho as a writer and assistant director in 1936, and worked his way up to the position of director. Beginning with the excellent *Rashomon*, Kurosawa made one classic film after the other, throughout the 1950s and 60s. These films were immensely appealing to international audiences, and this led to Kurosawa being criticised in his own country for making 'un-Japanese' films, designed to appeal to foreigners eager for orientalism. Kurosawa vigorously protested these criticisms, and rightly so. While he was more influenced by sources outside of Japan (such as Shakespeare and John Ford) than other Japanese directors, his films were also carefully constructed around Japanese artistic conventions. It is perhaps this combination of influences that makes Kurosawa's work so entertaining and accessible to world audiences.

Kurosawa's films are often moving stories about the individual, told with beautiful cinematography. In his long career, the Emperor, as he was nicknamed, proved he could make high-quality films in any genre. Whether it was romantic dramas like *Scandal*, medical dramas like *Red Beard* or cop films such as *Stray Dog*, Kurosawa always excelled, creating instant classics.

Kurosawa's influence on samurai films cannot be overstated. His wonderful *Seven Samurai* signified a new type of film for the genre, and the immensely successful *Yojimbo* and *Sanjuro* were such influential films that they completely transformed the genre in the 1960s.

HIROSHI INAGAKI

Another major Toho Studios director, Hiroshi Inagaki's work is also quite well known internationally. Inagaki specialised in historical epics, telling the stories of famous samurai and daimyo from times past. He excelled in the epic filmmaking that such projects required, as evidenced by films including *Samurai Trilogy*, *The 47 Ronin* and *Samurai Banners*. Inagaki was also very adept at filming large-scale battles, utilising great numbers of extras. His films are impressive for their epic scale, but also have a simple elegance about them.

MASAKI KOBAYASHI

A director famous for his distinctly anti-authoritarian films, Masaki Kobayashi made some of the most harrowingly honest samurai films; unlike many of his contemporaries, Kobayashi was much less sentimental about bushido, and was unafraid to show the potential for cruelty in the samurai's code of unquestioning loyalty and obedience. His films are usually concerned with the individual's struggle against corrupt authority, and never fail to be compelling viewing.

Drafted into the Japanese army during World War Two, Kobayashi served in Manchuria. He disapproved strongly of the war, and constantly refused promotion in the military. As the war came to an end, Kobayashi spent a year as a P.O.W. When back in Japan he returned to work for Shochiku Studios, utilising his wartime experiences to make *The Human Condition* trilogy, which told the harrowing story of a pacifist drafted into the Japanese army during World War Two. These films made Tatsuya Nakadai famous, and Kobayashi and Nakadai would continue to work together in a very successful partnership.

Unfortunately, Kobayashi's anti-authoritarian themes were not popular with Shochiku Studios, a very conservative company. Although a very talented director, Kobayashi made only 22 films.

Although not as influential as the work of Akira Kurosawa, Kobayashi's samurai films are distinct for their honesty and lack of sentimentalism; *Hara-kiri* especially shows the cruel realities of the bushido code. They are not only distinct in thematic content, but also for their extremely high quality. His direction is always sublime, and his choice of subject matter compelling and moving. His *Hara-kiri* and *Samurai Rebellion* rank alongside the work of Kurosawa as two of the finest samurai films ever made.

HIDEO GOSHA

Hideo Gosha originally worked in television, starting as a reporter with Nippon Television in 1953. He eventually secured a position as a director and producer with Fuji Television, where he created a series of successful action TV shows during the 1950s. One of these shows, *Three Outlaw Samurai*, impressed Shochiku Studios so much that they hired Gosha to make a feature-length version. Gosha continued to work with Shochiku Studios, directing many films throughout the 1960s and 70s, mainly of the samurai and yakuza (gangster) genres.

As Patrick Galloway has noted, Gosha blended elements of Kurosawa and Kobayashi's films with his fast-paced TV-style direction, to create a unique style of his own. This results in highly entertaining films, distinct from those of other master directors. Gosha's films are tremendous, and a wonderful addition to the samurai film genre.

Unfortunately, although famous and much loved in Japan, Gosha's films are yet to be widely available elsewhere, unlike the other directors profiled here. At the time of writing the Criterion release of *Sword of the Beast* on DVD is the only example of a large distributor with a Gosha film in their catalogue. This is a terrible shame, as Gosha's films are of a very high quality, and would be thoroughly enjoyed by international audiences. *Three Outlaw Samurai*, *Hunter in the Dark* and *Bandits vs. Samurai Squadron* are all available (with English subtitles) from importers, who source their stock from Asian distributors. Unfortunately, the quality of these DVDs is often inferior to those of the larger distributors (such as the Criterion Collection in the USA or Eastern Eye in Australia), but on the plus side they are a lot cheaper. It is definitely worth tracking these films down.

KIHACHI OKAMOTO

Like Masaki Kobayashi, Kihachi Okamoto was drafted into the Japanese army during World War Two, an experience which undoubtedly had an effect on his films in later years.

Beginning work for Toho Studios in 1947, Okamoto slowly worked his way up the ladder, directing his first film in 1958. Although he showed skill in directing films of various genres, Okamoto began to specialise in action films. He had a special talent for action scenes, which he was able to inject with a wonderful sense of rhythm and pacing, without over-stylising the violence.

Like Kobayashi, Okamoto was sceptical of the bushido code in his samurai films, but not in Kobayashi's anti-authoritarian way. Okamoto's films focus more on the individual, rather than the individual vs. authority. His samurai films often resemble cautionary tales, showing the ultimately negative and self-destructive results of leading a violent lifestyle. The best examples of this are the very gritty *Samurai Assassin* and *Sword of Doom* and the black comedy, *Kill!*. Okamoto's films combine his well-paced direction with moving subject matter, creating a result which clearly places him among the best samurai film directors.

THE STARS

TOSHIRO MIFUNE

Toshiro Mifune is not only the most well-known performer to appear in a samurai film, but also the most famous actor to emerge from Japanese cinema.

Mifune's acting career began with an audition for Toho Studios in 1946. Having served in the Japanese army during World War Two, Mifune found himself in need of work, and decided to use his military experience as an aerial photographer to attempt to secure work as a camera operator at one of the major studios in Tokyo. There are a number of different accounts as to how Mifune ended up auditioning as an actor; one claims he did so in the hope of later transferring to become a camera operator, another that he was to be interviewed for a position as a cameraman, but auditioned as an actor by mistake (which certainly makes a better story). Whatever the case, the audition process angered Mifune. He felt demeaned by requests to show different emotions and flew into a wild rage, the expressive nature of which impressed Kajiro Yamamoto, one of Toho's leading directors at the time, and an upcoming talent, Akira Kurosawa.

Mifune's angry audition secured him work as an actor, beginning with roles in comedies and action films. His long association with Akira Kurosawa began with *Drunken Angel*, in which his originally small part was expanded into a co-starring role. Mifune's relationship with Kurosawa continued throughout the 1940s, with leading roles in classic films such as *Stray Dog* and *Rashomon*. His explosive entry to the samurai film genre came with Kurosawa's masterpiece, *Seven Samurai*. Mifune brought a level of energy and expressiveness to all of these films, which Kurosawa was able to exploit to maximum effect. Between 1948 and 1965 Mifune had lead roles in 16 of Kurosawa's films, each one an instant classic.

Mifune also worked with many other Japanese directors, and as his films were successfully distributed internationally he secured roles in productions from other countries, most notably *Hell in the Pacific* and the hugely popular American samurai TV series *Shogun*, in 1980. He also started his own production company in the 1960s.

Toshiro Mifune had an enormous influence on the samurai film genre. Most of his characters, in particular Sanjuro (*Yojimbo*) and Kikuchiyo (*Seven Samurai*), were instant icons, and Mifune's unique portrayal was quickly copied by other actors. Only Shintaro Katsu and Tatsuya Nakadai come close to having the same level of influence.

TATSUYA NAKADAI

Tatsuya Nakadai is best known among fans of samurai films for his appearances in some of the genre's best films, such as *Yojimbo*, *Sanjuro*, *Hara-kiri*, *Kill!* and, perhaps his greatest of all, *Sword of Doom*.

Born in Tokyo in 1932, Nakadai worked in theatre before making the transition to film in 1953. His work with the Shingeki movement, a modern (rather than traditional) theatre group, rendered Nakadai with considerable acting experience before he was discovered by film director Masaki Kobayashi. Working for Shochiku Studios, Kobayashi used Nakadai in many of his films, most notably in *The Human Condition*, a challenging trilogy telling the story of a conscientious objector drafted into the Japanese army during World War Two.

By 1960 Nakadai had appeared in numerous Shochiku films, but his greatest samurai film roles were yet to come. Interestingly, Nakadai makes a very brief appearance in the best-known samurai film of all, *Seven Samurai*. In the early stages of the film, Nakadai is one of the samurai glimpsed striding through town.

Throughout the 1960s, Nakadai gave many memorable performances in samurai films such as *Hara-kiri*, *Yojimbo*, *Sanjuro*, *Sword of Doom*, *Kill!* and *Samurai Rebellion*. These roles ranged from tortured anti-heroes to sadistic villains, and Nakadai's excellent performance in each is testament to his impressive range.

Nakadai continues to work. He runs his own actors studio, *Mumeijuko*, and also appears in films, on television and on the stage.

SHINTARO KATSU

Most famous for his role as Zatoichi the blind swordsman, Shintaro Katsu was a huge star in Japan throughout the 1960s and 70s. Katsu was born into the acting profession, his family a successful kabuki (traditional Japanese theatre) troupe. In the 1950s he made the transition to cinema, working for Daiei Studios. His role as Zatoichi in the 1960s made him immensely popular, and the Zatoichi series continued into the 1970s and 80s. Katsu's warm and charismatic performance as the blind swordsman endeared him to audiences, but he was also capable of many other roles, such as the cruel villain he played in *Incident at Blood Pass*.

Katsu formed his own production company, which produced the popular *Lone Wolf and Cub* series, starring his older brother, Tomisaburo Wakayama.

THE INFLUENCE OF SAMURAI FILMS ON WORLD CINEMA

The influence the samurai film has had on world cinema is unquestionable. Themes from samurai films have been adopted both directly and indirectly by Hollywood; the never-ending *American Ninja* series of films (1985–1993) and recent would-be blockbuster *The Last Samurai* (2003) are both good examples of this. The relationship samurai films have with Hollywood's most famous genre, the western, is a bit more complicated. Some classic westerns owe their origins to samurai films: Kurosawa's *Seven Samurai* was remade as *The Magnificent Seven* (1960), while *Yojimbo* was remade by Sergio Leone in Italy as *A Fistful of Dollars* (1964), beginning the popular spaghetti western genre. It should be noted, however, that Kurosawa, the man who invented the modern samurai film, lists John Ford, the master of the classic western, as one of his influences. Kurosawa was able to create something unique, using Ford's films as one of his many inspirations. His work would then have a similar effect on directors of westerns in the 1960s. The samurai and western genres clearly share a very close relationship, but are distinct enough that they should remain separate.

The influence of samurai films in Hollywood was not limited to westerns. Many contemporary directors have a great deal of admiration for samurai films, and this has influenced their work in a variety of other genres. George Lucas's original *Star Wars* film, *A New Hope* (1977), was inspired in part by Kurosawa's *The Hidden Fortress*. Similarly, Quentin

Tarantino's *Kill Bill Volume 1* (2003) and *Volume 2* (2004) borrow heavily from samurai films, specifically *Lady Snowblood*. It is not only mainstream American films which have been influenced by the genre. Jim Jarmusch, a highly acclaimed alternative director, made his own tribute to samurai films, titled *Ghost Dog: The Way of the Samurai* (1999), an interesting film placing the samurai's unique moral code in the context of a modern American mob assassin.

BEGINNINGS AND THE 1950s

The samurai film evolved from some of the earliest Japanese films, which were filmed kabuki theatre performances. A traditional form of Japanese theatre, kabuki features carefully choreographed movements set to music and singing. Although graceful and beautiful, kabuki choreography is highly stylised, and lacks the sense of realism that films are able to convey.

It was another form of theatre choreography which would lead to the birth of the samurai film. The Shinkokugeki school of popular theatre, which had been around since 1912, distinguished itself with realistic and athletic swordplay, a stark contrast to the slow and graceful choreography of the filmed kabuki performances. The more realistic and faster-paced stage fencing had proven popular with audiences, and Makino Shozo, a highly successful producer of filmed kabuki performances, saw the potential of the Shinkokugeki productions and began to make films using their choreography and actors. Throughout the 1920s and 30s Japanese filmmakers began to explore the full potential of film as a medium, and the filmed kabuki performances were gradually replaced by narratives which were actually designed for the screen, rather than for the stage. Among these films were the early samurai films, which were popular with Japanese audiences. It would take another 20 years for the genre to be discovered by international audiences.

Samurai films suffered greatly in the 1940s and early 50s. Interestingly, they were suppressed by both the World War Two militaristic Japanese government, who considered them a useless form of entertainment, and the American post-war occupation censors, who maintained the often violent samurai films would inspire feudalistic sentiments among the Japanese. This caused a large decline in the production of samurai films, which was only reversed when the Japanese production companies were completely released from American censorship in the early 1950s.

One company quick to take advantage of this was Toei, an already successful studio. They began to mass produce samurai films, with great success, and were quickly copied by other studios. Unfortunately the years of suppression and censorship had left their mark on the genre. As Mitsuhiro Yoshimoto† has pointed out, many of the films made in the 1950s were extremely formulaic, and revolved around simplistic battles between good and evil. Also, they had restored the kabuki choreography for the sword-fighting scenes, resulting in very slow, dance-like choreography.

There were, however, some excellent samurai films made during the 1950s. Many directors tried to break the predictable formula which had such a tight grip on the genre. Hiroshi Inagaki was one such director, who created his highly acclaimed *Samurai Trilogy* during the 1950s. Telling the exciting story of master swordsman Miyamoto Musashi (an historical figure), Inagaki's films utilised swift and realistic choreography.

Akira Kurosawa was another innovator, and is the master filmmaker who would have the most influence on the genre. His 1954 film, *Seven Samurai*, was the beginnings of the samurai film as we know it today. As Yoshimoto has pointed out, in *Seven Samurai* Kurosawa created a very different kind of samurai film. Working for Toho, a company which had not made many samurai films, and didn't feel constrained by the existing formula, Kurosawa injected a level of realism and detail into his film which clearly set it apart. Character motivations were carefully

† Mitsuhiro Yoshimoto's highly informative work, *Kurosawa: Film Studies and Japanese Cinema*, contains a fascinating, in-depth discussion of the evolution of the jidaigeki genre, and is the source of the information in this summary.

thought out at the scripting stage, and every detail of the production design was researched to convey the sense of realism clearly lacking in many 1950s samurai films. The battle scenes in the film were also brutally realistic, with characters battling feverishly for their survival, rather than engaging in symbolic dance. Kurosawa continued to make high-quality samurai films throughout the 1950s, with *Throne of Blood* and *The Hidden Fortress*.

The work of both Inagaki and Kurosawa was well received overseas, and with their films the samurai film genre found an international audience.

Seven Samurai (1954)

Japanese Title: *Shichinin no samurai*
Directed by: Akira Kurosawa
Written by: Shinobu Hashimoto, Hideo Oguni, Akira Kurosawa
Produced by: Sojiro Motoki
Edited by: Akira Kurosawa
Cinematography: Asakazu Nakai
Cast: Takashi Shimura (Kambei), Toshiro Mifune (Kikuchiyo), Yoshio Inaba (Gorobei), Seiji Miyaguchi (Kyuzo), Minoru Chiaki (Heihachi), Daisuke Kato (Shichiroji), Isao Kimura (Katsushiro), Keiko Tsushima (Shino), Yukiko Shimazaki (Rikichi's wife), Kamatari Fujiwara (Manzo), Yoshio Kosugi (Mosuke), Bokuzen Hidari (Yohei), Yoshio Tsuchiya (Rikichi), Kokuten Kodo (Gisaku)

PLOT SUMMARY

Discovering that bandits will return to their village next harvest, some peasants set about hiring unemployed samurai, in the hope that they will defend their village. They find Kambei, an experienced and charismatic warrior, who not only takes on the assignment, but helps gather six other samurai. Among these is Kikuchiyo, a particularly messy and unkempt individual, who is drawn to the group and accepted mainly out of pity. Relations between the samurai and villagers are tense at best, neither group fully trusting the other. More stress is placed on this relationship when Katsushiro, the youngest of the seven, and Shino, a young peasant girl, fall in love with each other. Kikuchiyo turns out to be the key to maintaining the alliance of samurai and peasant, as it is discovered that he is of peasant origin himself. In a series of violent exchanges the samurai are able to defeat the bandits, mainly through Kambei's intelligent use of tactics. But this comes at a cost; at the end of the film only Kambei and two other samurai survive. The love between Katsushiro and Shino must remain unfulfilled; the samurai are no longer needed and must move on.

ANALYSIS

Seven Samurai is the masterpiece by Akira Kurosawa that defined the samurai film as we know it today. The film is an accomplished mix of superb characterisation, well-executed battle scenes and observations on the class structure of feudal Japan.

The characterisation in *Seven Samurai* is exceptional, as we have come to expect from Kurosawa. Each of the seven samurai is shown to have different motivations for joining the group, and they have widely varying character traits. While all seven performances are of a very high standard, special mention must go to Takashi Shimura and Toshiro Mifune. Shimura is well cast as Kambei, the wise samurai who brings the seven together. Shimura's sensitive performance shows a balance of warmth, intelligence and martial prowess in Kambei, making it clear to the audience that he is ideally suited to hold the seven together. Kikuchiyo, a wild, uncontrollable ronin, is played by Mifune, whose expressive features and blustering manner are perfect for the overblown character he plays. Kurosawa and his writers allegedly worked out detailed past histories for each of the seven, which pays off in a script full of realistic dialogue and convincing motivations. As we watch the

The seven enjoy a light-hearted moment. *Seven Samurai* directed by Akira Kurosawa and produced by Sojiro Motoki for Toho Studios.

seven prepare the village against the oncoming assault by the bandits, we grow attached to them, as we would to real people.

Kurosawa uses the samurai's interaction with the peasants as a device for examining class issues. As with all of Kurosawa's films this is not executed in a heavy-handed way, but instead integrated seamlessly into the film. There is a constant interplay of trust and mistrust between the samurai and the peasants, most of which arises from the class gulf between the two groups, which ultimately the characters in the film fail to bridge. Not even the potential relationship between young samurai Katsushiro and peasant girl Shino is able to form a solid bond between the two classes. This relationship fails the test set out by the film, just as the alliance between samurai and peasant does; when the unusual conditions that necessitated the two groups living and working together have passed, they both fall back into their old (separate) ways. The film's ending, which highlights the inevitability of this revelation, is sad and moving to watch. The final scenes of Kambei and the survivors, surveying the graves of their fallen comrades, while the peasants ignore them and continue to work as they have done for centuries, makes clear the ultimate fragility of the samurai class, stripping any sense of victory from Kambei and his men.

Perhaps the greatest feature of *Seven Samurai* is the lengthy battle scenes which take place towards its end. After we have come to know Kurosawa's carefully drawn characters we watch them fight, and in some cases die, in some of the finest battle scenes of the era. The action between the samurai and the bandits is choreographed carefully to give a realistic impression of combat. The combatants strike wildly and as often as they can, doing whatever possible to fell their enemy and, more importantly, survive. The screams of the dying are intercut with shots of their bodies in the muddy village, showing the true results of violence. Kurosawa also makes good use of the bandits' guns. The gun shots are always surprising, catching the audience off guard, and are sometimes, but not always, followed by death, creating an uneasy sense of uncertainty throughout the film.

Seven Samurai was remade as a western in 1960, *The Magnificent Seven*, directed by John Sturges and starring Yul Brynner, along with a cast of legends from the western genre such as Eli Wallach, Charles Bronson, Steve McQueen and James Coburn. Kurosawa's plot translated well into the genre, and the film was immensely successful, spawning three sequels, all with basically the same story as the original.

THE VERDICT

An undisputed classic of the samurai genre, *Seven Samurai* is compulsory viewing which satisfies on all levels.

Samurai 1: Miyamoto Musashi (1954)

Japanese Title: *Miyamoto Musashi*
Directed by: Hiroshi Inagaki
Written by: Adapted by Tokuhei Wakao and Hiroshi Inagaki from the novel by Eiji Yoshikawa
Produced by: Kazuo Takimura
Edited by: Hideshi Ohi
Cinematography: Jun Yasumoto
Cast: Toshiro Mifune (Takezo/Musashi), Rentaro Mikuni (Matahachi), Kuroemon Onoe (Takuan), Kaoru Yachigusa (Otsu), Mariko Okada (Akemi), Mitsuko Mito (Oko), Eiko Miyoshi (Osugi), Akihiko Hirata (Seijuro Yoshioka)

PLOT SUMMARY

When they fight on the losing side at the Battle of Sekigahara, Takezo and Matahachi, two glory-hungry young men, are forced to hide from the enemy in a house occupied by two women: Oko and her daughter, Akemi. A fierce warrior, Takezo protects them from some bandits, but is driven away by the unwanted advances of both women. Oko lies to Matahachi, telling him that Musashi attempted to rape her, and convincing him to leave with her and Akemi. Takezo, meanwhile, has become a wanted fugitive, after a dispute with some border guards. Despite several attempts, including a trap set by Osugi, Matahachi's bitter mother, the authorities are unable to capture Takezo. The wise priest, Takuan, and Otsu, the fiancée Matahachi left behind, are finally able to subdue him. Takuan suspends Takezo from a tree, hoping to tame the wild young man with harsh discipline, but Otsu shows pity and releases him. Takezo is touched that someone would actually help him and begins to see the selfish nature of his wild ways. Otsu is captured by the authorities, and Takezo journeys to Himeji castle to rescue her.

There he is tricked by Takuan into beginning a rigorous moral education, and eventually becoming a samurai, renaming himself Musashi. Musashi is ordered to travel and train himself. He visits Otsu before he leaves, but decides he cannot take her with him, asking her to wait for him a little longer.

ANALYSIS

Miyamoto Musashi is a strong start to Hiroshi Inagaki's *Samurai Trilogy*, a series of films that tell the famous story of the historical figure who many consider to be Japan's greatest swordsman. A captivating story, told in a simple yet entertaining way, *Miyamoto Musashi* was well deserving of the Academy Award for Best Foreign Film that it won in 1955.

Miyamoto Musashi is perhaps the best example of director Hiroshi Inagaki's unique style. Along with cinematographer Jun Yasumoto, Inagaki uses a storytelling technique that is elegant in its simplicity. Taking advantage of the film's magnificent landscapes, Inagaki utilises slow pans across muddy battlefields, daunting mountains and beautiful meadows. Much more than pretty pictures (although, it must be noted, many of Inagaki and Yasumoto's shots would look fantastic framed on a wall), these shots also reveal important information. The shot of Takezo, running through a picturesque meadow, wooden sword in hand, violently chopping flowers off their stalks, perfectly captures his wild nature. Similarly, the priest Takuan, when attempting to capture Takezo, is clearly separated from the other would-be captors; in a shot taken from high in the mountains, he is in the foreground and the others in the background, far below him in a valley. Similarly, the beginning of the Battle of Sekigahara is signified by an atmospheric shot of lightning striking, illuminating a skeletal tree. Inagaki is a master of using simple images to convey information, one of the hallmarks of a great filmmaker.

Like *Seven Samurai*, *Miyamoto Musashi* not only contains some beautiful scenic shots, but also some very well-directed and atmospheric battle scenes. Like Kurosawa, Inagaki was an innovator when it came to presenting violence, and the battle scenes have a greater sense of realism than many of the 1950s samurai films. The Battle of Sekigahara scenes, although quite short, effectively convey the sense of confusion and brutality in warfare, through the use of a series of quick cuts, each shot filled with moving bodies, flailing wildly at each other. We find it difficult to pick out Takezo and Matahachi in these frenetic images, and just as we locate them, Inagaki cuts to another shot. The location – a muddy field with the occasional gnarled tree – complements the action.

The elegance and simplicity of Inagaki's direction is also present in the plot itself. An uncomplicated story about a powerful young man who learns the error of his wild ways, *Miyamoto Musashi* has a mythic and parabolic feel about it. Contained within the story are a number of beautiful moments between the characters, played with just the right amount of emotion. The scene when Takezo bandages Otsu's hands, injured when she freed him, is particularly touching, and shows him beginning to understand the needs of others. Similarly, Otsu's sad realisation that Musashi has left her behind is handled very well, and Toshiro Mifune and Kaoru Yachigusa should be commended for their skilful performances.

THE VERDICT

An excellent film in its own right, *Miyamoto Musashi* sets the tone of Hiroshi Inagaki's acclaimed *Samurai Trilogy*. Inagaki's beautiful direction, along with an entertaining story and solid performances from a great cast, make this a must-see for anyone interested in samurai films.

Samurai 2: Duel at Ichijoji Temple (1955)

Japanese Title: *Zoku Miyamoto Musashi: Ichijoji no ketto*
Directed by: Hiroshi Inagaki
Written by: Adapted by Tokuhei Wakao and Hiroshi Inagaki from the novel by Eiji Yoshikawa

Produced by: Kazuo Takimura
Edited by: Hideshi Ohi
Cinematography: Jun Yasumoto
Cast: Toshiro Mifune (Miyamoto/Takezo), Koji Tsuruta (Kojiro Sasaki), Kaoru Yachigusa (Otsu), Mariko Okada (Akemi), Michiyo Kogure (Lady Yoshino), Mitsuko Mito (Oku), Akihiko Hirata (Seijuro Yoshioka), Daisuke Kato (Toji), Kuroemon Onoe (Takuan), Sachio Sakai (Matahachi)

PLOT SUMMARY

Musashi has been travelling for a few years now, improving his swordsmanship, but he is yet to master the psychological strengths of the samurai. Arriving in Kyoto, Musashi begins a rivalry with the Yoshioka school of swordsmanship. He wants to challenge the master of the school, Seijuro, but is continually betrayed by the Yoshioka, who make two attempts to kill him with their superior numbers. Musashi visits a sword polisher, Koetsu, and begins to learn from him the benefits of emotional detachment when duelling. He also sees Otsu for the first time in years, but now desires the perfection of his art more than her. A sinister warrior, Kojiro Sasaki, witnesses Musashi's battle against the Yoshioka, and is impressed. Otsu is heartbroken, and returns to Takuan's monastery, where she considers becoming a nun. To avoid further confrontations with the Yoshioka, Musashi stays at a Geisha house, where Lady Yoshino teaches him the value of a gentle nature. After Musashi defeats Denshichiro, Seijuro's brother, the Yoshioka finally agree to a duel with Seijuro, at Ichijoji temple. The Yoshioka ambush him with 80 men, and Musashi fights bravely, killing many of his opponents before escaping. He sees Seijuro, who he defeats easily, but decides to spare him, considering the teachings of Koetsu and Yoshino. Wounded, Musashi is found by Otsu, who nurses him back to health. Musashi violently embraces Otsu, but she rejects him. Musashi continues on his lonely journey, watched by Kojiro, who hopes to have a match with him in the future…

ANALYSIS

Samurai 2: Duel at Ichijoji Temple is an enjoyable continuation of Hiroshi Inagaki's retelling of the life of Miyamoto Musashi, a famous swordsman from the pages of Japanese history. The film continues Musashi's learning journey as he becomes a samurai as well as a skilled warrior.

The exact nature of this journey is one of the unique aspects of the samurai film, and may seem unusual to western audiences. After all, it's hard to imagine the heroes of Hollywood films, such as the western or gangster genres, visiting a woman to learn etiquette and gentleness, as Musashi does. And yet, this is one of the film's most captivating features. The idea that a warrior can be cultured and skilled at killing at the same time is an interesting juxtaposition, which is explored very effectively here. It's not enough for Musashi to be a skilled swordsman; he must have a detachment from the world that eclipses his fear and murderous desires, one of the hallmarks of the samurai.

Director Hiroshi Inagaki uses slightly different techniques in this film than he did in *Miyamoto Musashi*. He again makes use of some spectacular scenery; the opening shots of Musashi walking along the road are particularly memorable. However, while the focus of the first film was on introducing the characters, something Inagaki uses the landscape for very effectively, *Duel at Ichijoji Temple* concerns the feud between Musashi and the Yoshioka school, and as such has a focus on battle scenes rather than picturesque landscapes. Inagaki also brings Musashi's writings into the film in a couple of brief scenes in which we see the shaping of his philosophy. These key moments contain the actual words of Musashi's works on screen, superimposed over the moment that Musashi chose that particular path. The best example of this is the scene in which Musashi, preparing for a major duel, goes to pray for his success. He stops himself and thinks carefully before deciding: 'I respect deities, but I do not rely on them'. These small moments offer an insight into the formation of Musashi's philosophy, and form a strong link between Inagaki's films and the real Musashi.

The battle scenes in this film are very effective. Interestingly, many of them appear to have been filmed in studio lots, rather than on location, as was the case for many scenes in *Miyamoto Musashi*. However, Inagaki makes use of the studio setting to inject some mood into the scenes, through the use of wind machines and effective lighting. A good example of this is the duel Musashi has at the beginning of the film, which takes place on a windy plain at night, an atmosphere created well in the studio environment; the battle itself is extremely tense and ends abruptly and unpredictably. The choreography of the battle scenes is also of a high standard, both fast and unpredictable. The film's climax – Musashi's battle with the 80 Yoshioka students – is also handled very well, and in a realistic manner. It is believable that Musashi could have defeated the 80 men, particularly when we see him venture into a rice paddy, in which his enemies are slowed down by the marsh-like conditions and forced to attack him one at a time.

THE VERDICT

Although very different to the first entry in the *Samurai Trilogy*, *Duel at Ichijoji Temple* is a very well-made film. Inagaki uses simple but effective techniques to present an entertaining story, offering interesting insights into the world of the warrior and some very well-choreographed battle scenes.

Samurai 3: Duel on Ganryu Island (1956)

Japanese Title: *Miyamoto Musashi kanketsuhen ketto Ganryujima*
Directed by: Hiroshi Inagaki
Written by: Adapted by Tokuhei Wakao and Hiroshi Inagaki from the novel by Eiji Yoshikawa
Produced by: Kazuo Takimura
Edited by: Hirokazu Iwashita
Cinematography: Kazuo Yamada

Cast: Toshiro Mifune (Miyamoto Musashi), Koji Tsuruta (Kojiro Sasaki), Kaoru Yachigusa (Otsu), Michiko Saga (Omitsu), Mariko Okada (Akemi), Takashi Shimura (Court Official), Minoru Chiaki (Sasuke)

PLOT SUMMARY

The story of Miyamoto Musashi continues... Musashi's reputation as a formidable samurai has spread, and Lord Yagyu, fencing instructor to the Shogun, invites him to Edo. Meanwhile Kojiro has also travelled to Edo and manages to secure a position with Hosokawa, a daimyo. Finding Musashi, Kojiro challenges him to a duel which Musashi first agrees to, and then postpones, explaining that he needs first to take a journey. Musashi, and his students, Jotaro and Kumagoro, journey to a small village which they help protect from bandits. Musashi rediscovers village life and enjoys it, no longer craving fame and fortune. The two women who love him, Otsu and Akemi, find Musashi at the village, and quickly renew their animosity. In a struggle, they accidentally light a fire, which draws bandits to the village. Akemi dies protecting Otsu, and Kumagoro is slain before the bandits are driven away. Musashi receives word from Kojiro that he is growing impatient for their duel and he leaves the village, despite Otsu begging him not to. The duel takes place at Ganryu island. Kojiro fights bravely, but is ultimately defeated by Musashi's superior skill. Realising Kojiro is the greatest swordsman he will ever face, Musashi weeps at the loss of such a man from the world.

ANALYSIS

Samurai 3: Duel on Ganryu Island is a fitting end to Hiroshi Inagaki's *Samurai Trilogy*. Inagaki combines his use of effective cinematography with a compelling story and well-choreographed battle scenes.

This film charts the final stages of Miyamoto Musashi's development; he is no longer obsessed with fame and instead has become the ultimate samurai, one who is more than simply strong and craves only to be the best he can at his chosen art. Developing his persona further, Musashi now prefers to settle matters peacefully, avoiding unnecessary violence on a few occasions throughout the film, most notably when he placates some angry thugs by swiftly plucking flies from the air with a pair of chop-sticks, intimidating them with his speed and accuracy. Musashi is contrasted to Kojiro, who is very ambitious, and seeks to make his reputation in the bloodiest way possible. The progression of Musashi's character over the trilogy sets each film clearly apart, and avoids the repetition of themes present in other film series.

With *Duel on Ganryu Island*, Hiroshi Inagaki again takes the opportunity to utilise some grand scenery, giving specific scenes an epic backdrop. The opening scene of Kojiro standing in front of a waterfall, a rainbow clearly visible in the mist, is a spectacular image. When we have finished admiring it, Inagaki quickly presents us with the sinister juxtaposition of Kojiro's cruelty (to Akemi and an unfortunate swallow). Similarly, the tense and protracted duel between Musashi and Kojiro takes place on a beach at sunrise, and has as its backdrop a striking image of the sun over the water; even in its more brutal moments, Inagaki's film has a certain elegance and beauty.

The performances achieve the typically high standard of the entire *Samurai Trilogy*. Koji Tsuruta is especially good as Kojiro, given many more opportunities to shine here than in the second film, where he appeared in only a few scenes. Tsuruta skilfully captures the sinister edge to Kojiro's character, giving a convincing impression of a man who craves the recognition that defeating Musashi would bring.

The film's climactic moment, the duel between Musashi and Kojiro, is handled particularly well. Mifune and Tsuruta both bring a level of intensity to this scene, which along with Inagaki's direction creates a tense atmosphere. Inagaki cuts between shots of Musashi and then Kojiro, showing the determination on each man's face. When the two actually clash, this is shown through quick cuts accompanied by the sound of the weapons meeting. Words do not do this sequence justice.

It is one of the greatest duels in any samurai film, a befitting reconstruction of one of the most famous duels in Japanese history.

THE VERDICT

Samurai 3: Duel on Ganryu Island is a highly satisfying conclusion to the *Samurai Trilogy*. In the fulfilment of Musashi's learning journey, we glean a lot about the ideals of the samurai. Inagaki's epic direction makes the entire trilogy essential viewing for any fan of samurai films.

Throne of Blood (1957)

Japanese Title: *Kumonosu jo*
Directed by: Akira Kurosawa
Written by: Adapted by Shinobu Hashimoto, Ryuzo Kikushima, Hideo Oguni and Akira Kurosawa from William Shakespeare's *Macbeth*
Produced by: Sojiro Motoki, Akira Kurosawa
Edited by: Akira Kurosawa
Cinematography: Asakazu Nakai
Cast: Toshiro Mifune (Washizu), Isuzu Yamada (Asaji), Takashi Nomura (Noriyasu), Akira Kubo (Miki), Yoichi Tachikawa (Tsuzuki), Minoru Chiaki (Yoshiaki), Takamaru Sasaki (Kuniharo), Chieko Naniwa (spirit)

PLOT SUMMARY

A daimyo's two finest samurai, Washizu and Miki, meet a spirit, which predicts they will both receive promotions and that Washizu will eventually become the new daimyo of the castle, succeeded by Miki's son. To their amazement, the first prediction becomes true and both Washizu and Miki are promoted to higher positions, each put in charge of an important fort. When Washizu's wife, Asaji, hears of the prediction, she urges him to fulfil the prophecy by murdering the daimyo. Although reluctant at first, Washizu performs the murder, and is nearly driven mad by guilt. Washizu and Asaji frame another samurai, Noriyasu, for the murder, who flees with the young prince. Washizu appoints Miki's son as his successor, securing his support, but changes his mind when Asaji tells him she is pregnant. Washizu orders some of his men to kill Miki and his son, and although Miki is slain, his son escapes. As Washizu is gradually driven mad by his deeds, his enemies begin to move against him. Noriyasu, the prince and Miki's son have allied themselves to Inui, a rival daimyo, and are marching on the castle. Worried, Washizu visits the spirit again, who assures him that he will not be defeated unless Spider Web Wood, the thick forest surrounding the castle, marches on him. Washizu is buoyed by confidence, and tells his men of the prophecy. When they see the moving forest, which Noriyasu and his men have cut down and are using as camouflage, they kill Washizu, hoping to surrender him to his enemies.

ANALYSIS

Throne of Blood is an excellent adaptation of Shakespeare's *Macbeth*, which benefits from superb direction by Akira Kurosawa. Shakespeare's dark tale proves to be a perfect match for Kurosawa's atmospheric story-telling. Kurosawa and his staff of writers make quite a few changes to Shakespeare's tale, but the same basic story of a man undone by his own ambition is present in the film, and the many inspired scenes in *Throne of Blood*, particularly those at the end, would never have been filmed if Kurosawa had stuck strictly to the original story.

The most outstanding aspect of *Throne of Blood* is Kurosawa's use of cinematic techniques to create atmosphere. The film opens with a view of a fog-shrouded plain. We hear the slow deliberate lyrics of a Japanese song, lamenting man's inability to escape ambition and violence. Through the fog, a memorial comes into view, revealing that a castle once stood here. The memorial is engulfed in thick fog, which slowly clears to reveal the castle, back in the time when it still stood. This has to be one of the greatest beginnings to a samurai film, or, for that matter,

Spider Web Castle. *Throne of Blood* directed by Akira Kurosawa and produced by Sojiro Motoki and Akira Kurosawa for Toho Studios.

any film. Kurosawa captures the themes of Shakespeare's play in a few evocative images, and catapults us into his film; we already know the castle is doomed to be destroyed, a fate which, we later discover, will be shared by the film's tragic central character.

Kurosawa continues this highly evocative use of images and sound throughout his film. The scene in which Washizu and Miki meet the spirit is particularly creepy; the spirit sits, completely pale, and doesn't move, except to continually weave silk on a Japanese spinning wheel. The interior of the spirit's hovel is also completely white, and the whole scene is bathed in a white light which gives it a stark appearance, like the billowing fog or the bleached bones we see a moment later. Similarly, the sounds of Washizu's wife, Asaji, as she moves are sinister, the impression intensified when it becomes clear just how ruthless she is. The way her kimono makes a quiet shuffling sound as she moves across the bare boards of her home grows increasingly chilling throughout the early moments of the film. When Asaji fetches some poisoned sake, we see her disappear into a darkened room, vanishing into the darkness. The sounds of her kimono dragging on the floor grow quieter and then slowly louder as she returns, sake pot in hand, walking straight towards the camera.

Kurosawa's evocative direction is coupled with one of Toshiro Mifune's most memorable performances. In his leading role as Washizu, Mifune presents a picture of a man slowly going mad; from his stunned, statue-like appearance after he has killed his lord, through his manic confidence, to his despair at the film's end, Mifune's performance is an unnerving portrayal of a man who loses everything to ambition. Isuzu Yamada is also unnervingly convincing in her role as Asaji. She is cold

Washizu (Toshiro Mifune) under attack. *Throne of Blood* directed by Akira Kurosawa and produced by Sojiro Motoki and Akira Kurosawa for Toho Studios.

and inexpressive in many of her scenes, as she encourages her husband to murder first his lord, and then his closest friend. Ultimately, she too succumbs to the horror of what she and her husband have done, and Yamada portrays this well, in the classic *Macbeth* hand-washing scene.

Throne of Blood gains most of its dramatic mileage from atmospheric storytelling, rather than frenetic action, but this film contains one of the most distinct and memorable action scenes of any samurai film. The scene in which Washizu's men turn on him, attempting to kill him with vast numbers of arrows, is particularly striking. Washizu frantically runs from one side of a balcony to the other, arrows thudding into the wood around him. His death scene, although bloodless, has to be one of the most shocking seen in any samurai film.

THE VERDICT

Throne of Blood is a classic fusion of an archetypical story with highly skilled direction and performances. One of Kurosawa's finest films, and an example of the samurai film at its best.

The Hidden Fortress (1958)

Japanese Title: *Kakushi-toride no san-akunin*
Directed by: Akira Kurosawa
Written by: Adapted by Shinobu Hashimoto, Ryuzo Kikushima, Hideo Oguni and Akira Kurosawa from the novel by Shugoro Yamamoto
Produced by: Akira Kurosawa, Masumi Fujimoto
Edited by: Akira Kurosawa
Cinematography: Ichio Yamazeki
Cast: Toshiro Mifune (General Rokurota Makabe), Misa Uehara (Princess Yuki of the Akizuki clan), Minoru Chiaki (Tahei), Kamatari Fujiwara (Matashichi), Takashi Shimura (Izumi Nagakura), Susumu Fujita (General Hyoe Tadakoro), Toshiko Higuchi (girl bought from brothel owner)

PLOT SUMMARY

Two peasant prisoners of war, Matashichi and Tahei, escape the Yamana clan and discover the hidden fortune of the defeated Akizuki clan. The two peasants are found by General Rokurota, who, along with Princess Yuki and the gold, is staying in the Akizuki hidden fortress, a building carefully concealed in the mountains. Princess Yuki and the gold are both wanted badly by the Yamana, and Rokurota needs to get them safely to the friendly Hayakawa clan. Hearing Matashichi and Tahei's bold plan to actually travel through Yamana territory to get to Hayakawa, Rokurota decides to go with them. He ensures the peasants' help by promising them a share of the gold. The high-spirited Princess Yuki pretends to be a mute peasant girl, as the unusual group sets out on their journey, carrying a cargo of gold, hidden in pieces of firewood. Narrowly avoiding capture many times, Rokurota and Yuki are eventually caught by their enemies. They escape execution with the help of Hyoe Tadakoro, a Yamana general who is impressed by Yuki's spirit and leadership. Safely in Hayakawa territory, Yuki rewards the peasants with a small trinket. Grateful to have escaped with their lives, the two friends head home.

ANALYSIS

By far the most commercial of Akira Kurosawa's films, *The Hidden Fortress* is nonetheless an exciting adventure, featuring impressive and well-realised scenes, on a much larger scale than any of his previous films.

Kurosawa makes good use of the widescreen format (this is his first widescreen film) and a large budget to tell an epic story. Legions of extras are utilised to create convincing armies on the march, army encampments and a huge peasant procession. Among these scenes is a frenetic sequence depicting a riot, as prisoners of war attempt to escape. Kurosawa fills a darkened screen with writhing bodies as the prisoners swarm over their guards, suggesting the horror and confusion of violence on a large scale.

The scenes in which Princess Yuki and General Rokurota are pursued by large numbers of enemy troops are also worthy of mention, helped along by sombre music as the Yamana troops march through the forest. The action scenes throughout *The Hidden Fortress* are also of a high quality, particularly the spear fight between Rokurota and Hyoe. The two battle all over a Yamana camp in a fast-paced and exciting scene.

The cast of this film all perform admirably. The beautiful Misa Uehara brings a nice level of haughtiness to the high-spirited Princess Yuki, while Toshiro Mifune is flawless as the stern Rokurota, giving a slight promise of his future, influential performance in *Yojimbo*. Susumu Fujita and Toshiko Higuchi also perform very well in their respective roles.

Interestingly, despite the large numbers of extras used for lavish staging, the most influential element of *The Hidden Fortress* is the way much of the story is told from the perspective of the two peasants, Matashichi and Tahei. The constant bickering between these two characters is always amusing, particularly in the way they always seem to forget all their petty arguments the moment trouble looms. Minoru Chiaki and Kamatari Fujiwara are to be commended for the energy they bring to their roles; despite their obvious greed the peasants come across as likeable characters. Much of the humour in the film comes from the way these two interact with both each other and the remaining characters. The scene in which Matashichi and Tahei attempt to convince Princess Yuki, who they believe is deaf and mute, that they want to take her gold-laden horse for a drink, is particularly amusing as the two engage in increasingly stupid sign language, all the while bickering over who is doing a better job.

However, the two peasant characters do not only provide comic relief. They also allow the audience a way into the film. *The Hidden Fortress* tells a story of royalty and generals, of big events involving important people. While exciting, such stories are often difficult for audiences to relate to, as they have little in common with the central characters. In Matashichi and Tahei, writers Shinobu Hashimoto and Ryuzo Kikushima give the audience two regular guys, just trying to get along in life, something most of us can easily relate to.

It was this element of *The Hidden Fortress* that had a large influence on world cinema. George Lucas has stated that the film was one of his main inspirations when writing the script for *Star Wars: A New Hope*. In particular, the characters of Matashichi and Tahei inspired him to tell his story largely from the perspective of two seemingly unimportant characters caught up in big events, the two droids, R2-D2 and C3P0. The characters of Leia and Obi Wan Kenobi also bear a slight resemblance to Yuki and Rokurota. Lucas has stated that earlier versions of the script of *Star Wars: A New Hope* actually contained scenes in which Leia and Obi Wan were making their way through enemy territory, as Yuki and Rokurota do in *The Hidden Fortress*.

THE VERDICT

The Hidden Fortress is a very enjoyable adventure film, utilising widescreen photography and large, well-staged scenes to tell an epic story. Worth seeing alone for the amusing characterisation of Matashichi and Tahei.

Samurai Saga (1959)

Japanese Title: *Aru kengo no shogai*
Directed by: Hiroshi Inagaki
Written by: Adapted by Hiroshi Inagaki from Edmond Rostand's, *Cyrano de Bergerac*
Produced by: Tomoyuki Tanaka
Edited by: Kazuji Taira
Cinematography: Kazuo Yamada
Cast: Toshiro Mifune (Heihachiro Komaki), Yoko Tsukasa (Lady Ochii), Akira Takarada (Jurota Karibe), Seizaburo Kawazu (Lord Nagashima),

Kamatari Fujiwara (Rakuzo, owner of the sake house), Akihiko Hirata (Akaboshi), Keiko Awaji (Nanae), Eiko Miyoshi (Okuni)

PLOT SUMMARY

Komaki, a boisterous warrior with a large nose, is in love with Lady Ochii, his childhood friend, but she loves a handsome young samurai named Jurota. Putting aside his own wishes, Komaki helps Jurota woo Ochii by writing him romantic poems to recite. This works for a while, and culminates in Komaki making an impassioned speech to Ochii, declaring his love for her, from the cover of darkness outside her window. Ochii believes Jurota to have made this speech and embraces him, but before their relationship can develop any further war breaks out. At the Battle of Sekigahara Komaki and Jurota fight on the losing side and they narrowly escape the battlefield. Realising Komaki's words are what Ochii really loves, Jurota urges him to make it back to her safely, committing suicide so as not to slow him down. Ten years pass and Ochii has become a nun. Komaki continues to visit her, but he is found by the Tokugawa, who still hunt him. Tricked into a cowardly ambush, Komaki receives a fatal blow to his head. He manages to visit Ochii one last time as he dies, and as she hears him read to her, she realises it was Komaki who made that speech at her window. Komaki faces death bravely, regretful that he was killed in such a dishonourable fashion, but determined not to lose his indomitable spirit.

ANALYSIS

An adaptation of Edmond Rostand's play *Cyrano de Bergerac*, *Samurai Saga* makes use of some interesting subject matter. The material works very well in the context of a samurai film, and director Hiroshi Inagaki should be commended for utilising such unusual material.

Inagaki is able to capture both the pathos and humour present in Rostand's play. Toshiro Mifune's energetic performance as Komaki adds humour to the scenes where he and others make fun of his unusually large nose. Worthy of mention is a scene early in the film when Komaki disrupts a kabuki performance. Angered, Lord Nagashima's samurai attempt to insult Komaki, but he beats them to it, making fun of his own nose in an exaggerated performance, which is very amusing. Komaki then goes on to defeat Nagashima's men on the stage, composing a song as he does so. Inagaki and his actors are able to bring just the right amount of pathos to the more dramatic scenes of *Samurai Saga*, without descending into melodrama. The final scenes of the film are handled very well by Toshiro Mifune and Yoko Tsukasa, whose convincing performances make Kamaki and Ochii's fate all the more tragic.

The cinematography in *Samurai Saga* is up to the usual high standards of Inagaki's films, containing many memorable images. Inagaki and Mifune handle Komaki's death scene especially well; he challenges death among the falling petals of a cherry tree, creating a beautiful image, evocatively capturing the sadness and inevitability of the act.

The action scenes in *Samurai Saga* are quite unusual, and accompany a tonal shift in the film itself. The action that takes place in the first half of the film is largely comedic and bloodless, such as Komaki's amusing humiliation of Nagashima's samurai on the kabuki stage, and Jurota's battle with a large group of samurai, watched gleefully by Komaki. No one is hurt in these scenes; fallen samurai simply get to their feet and run away. This all changes after the Battle of Sekigahara sequence, which utilises some of the gritty battle scenes shot for *Miyamoto Musashi*. The scenes where Komaki, Jurota and other survivors of the losing side are gunned down by Nagashima's troops are brutal by comparison. The choreography of Komaki's last battle is also a contrast to the earlier scenes; he dodges among alleys, using the close quarters to dispatch his multiple opponents one at a time, and, in these scenes, they actually stay dead.

This shift in tone is very effective. Inagaki creates a gentler, whimsical mood in the first half of his film, which is shattered by the war and its subsequent violence. The earlier comedic violence causes the audience to let their guard down, which makes the real violence all the more effective.

THE VERDICT

Cyrano de Bergerac, samurai style. In the hands of a skilled director like Hiroshi Inagaki this works very well, and proves the flexibility of the genre.

THE 1960s

The 1960s saw an explosion of excellent samurai films, which forever changed the genre. This trend was brought about by Akira Kurosawa and two of his early 1960s films, *Yojimbo* and *Sanjuro*. Both starred Toshiro Mifune as Sanjuro, a ronin with a wry sense of humour and a quick draw. They featured graphic violence as it had never before been seen in samurai films; arms were cut off and shown falling to the ground, and in one particularly notable scene, blood spurts in a fine mist from the chest of one of Sanjuro's fallen opponents. Furthermore, Kurosawa's films had a wonderfully dark sense of humour, with Sanjuro fashioned as a callous but immensely likeable anti-hero. The moments of violence were used sparingly and to great effect in Kurosawa's films, and clearly audiences approved. *Yojimbo* and *Sanjuro* were both very successful commercially, so much so that Toei and the other companies were forced to take notice.

The commercial success of Kurosawa's work meant that the 1960s samurai films were free of the formulaic plots and slow choreography that had plagued many throughout the 1950s. This shift in focus ensured their popularity throughout the 1960s, with many released each year. This gave directors such as Kenji Misumi, Kihachi Okamoto, Masaki Kobayashi and Hideo Gosha a great deal more freedom, and resulted in consistently high-quality films throughout the 1960s. These samurai films were characterised by Sanjuro-style anti-heroism and graphic violence, but many also told moving stories, and were far more than the simple genre films they appeared to be.

The 1960s also gave birth to Daiei studio's famous Zatoichi series. Featuring a highly skilled blind swordsman, these films benefited from a novel concept, a variety of good directors and writers, and leading man Shintaro Katsu's very likeable portrayal of Zatoichi. The original Zatoichi series would last into the 1980s (Katsu starring in every film), and was highly influential, spawning many imitators.

Yojimbo (1961)

Japanese Title: *Yojimbo*
Directed by: Akira Kurosawa
Written by: Ryuzo Kikushima, Akira Kurosawa
Produced by: Ryuzo Kikushima, Tomoyuki Tanaka, Akira Kurosawa
Edited by: Akira Kurosawa
Cinematography: Kazuo Miyagawa
Cast: Toshiro Mifune (Sanjuro), Tatsuya Nakadai (Unosuke), Yoko Tsukasa (Nui), Isuzu Yamada (Orin), Daisuke Kato (Inokichi), Seizaburo Kawazu (Seibei), Takashi Shimura (Tokuemon), Eijiro Tono (Gonji), Atsushi Watanabe (coffin-maker)

PLOT SUMMARY

Sanjuro, a ronin, arrives at a small town, and begins to provoke conflict between two criminal gangs, hoping they'll wipe each other out, cleaning up the town. One of the gangs is led by Seibei and his cruel wife, Orin. The other is led by Ushi-Tora and his two brothers, Inokichi, a fool, and Unosuke, a sadistic man who uses a modern revolver instead of a sword. Sanjuro pretends to work as a bodyguard for both gangs, making them compete for his services. When Sanjuro frees a captive woman, Nui, who's important to Ushi-Tora's gang, his machinations are undone. Unosuke discovers Sanjuro's treachery, and has him badly beaten by his thugs. Meanwhile, Ushi-Tora and his brothers eliminate Seibei and his gang in a surprise attack. Using his cunning to escape his captors, Sanjuro is taken to a temple to recover by Gonji, a grizzled old tavern owner who despises the gangs and what they've done to his town. When Gonji is taken captive and tortured by Ushi-Tora, Sanjuro returns to the town, and challenges Ushi-Tora and his gang. In the bloody battle that ensues, Sanjuro defeats the entire gang. Satisfied his work is done, the ronin moves on.

ANALYSIS

1961 audiences must have known they were in for something different when they settled down to the opening scenes of *Yojimbo*. The film has a feel and tone which are almost the complete opposite of the far gentler samurai films of the 1950s. In the first reel of *Yojimbo* we see a stray dog running through a dirty street, a decaying human hand in its mouth, and Sanjuro severing the arm of a thug, which we see fall to the ground. Used to the gentle, gore-free choreography of the 1950s films, Japanese audiences would have been unaccustomed to such images.

Also, the potent tone director Akira Kurosawa brings to *Yojimbo* would have been largely new and fresh to Japanese audiences. The town Sanjuro wanders into is desolate and barren, free from any life except the aforementioned dog and the nasty thugs of two rival criminal gangs. The only person enjoying himself is the coffin-maker, whose business has never been better. Kurosawa matches the desolate appearance of the town with swift and graphic violence throughout *Yojimbo*; aside from the severed arm, we see gang members murder their enemies as they flee a burning house, and the film's climactic ending is far bloodier than any samurai film before it.

Despite *Yojimbo*'s reputation for violence, scenes of brutality are actually used quite sparingly in the film, with relatively few such moments appearing in comparison to other 1960s samurai films, or even Kurosawa's earlier work, *Seven Samurai*. The graphic scenes, spread throughout, are used to punctuate key moments, often sudden and

Sanjuro (Toshiro Mifune) in action. *Yojimbo* directed by Akira Kurosawa and produced by Ryuzo Kikushima, Tomoyuki Tanaka and Akira Kurosawa for Toho Studios.

unexpected, so the audience doesn't become desensitised to their effect.

Amazingly, Kurosawa is able to blend this sombre, violent tone with humour to create a very effective black comedy. Sanjuro himself has an unusual wit, and his callousness makes much of the film darkly funny; after killing three thugs he casually remarks to the coffin-maker that he should make three more coffins. Worthy of mention is Inokichi (Daisuke Kato), brother of Ushi-Tora, the leader of one of the rival gangs. Inokichi is very stupid, and the scene in which he is tricked into helping carry a badly beaten Sanjuro (who is hidden in a coffin) to safety is made hilarious by the exuberance Daisuke Kato brings to the role. Perhaps the moment which best epitomises the thread of humour running through *Yojimbo* is when Sanjuro, badly beaten and scarred around his face, attempts to reassure Gonji that he is alright by smiling. The image of Toshiro Mifune's face, made up with open wounds and dark bruises, with a huge smile, is disturbing yet funny, particularly when Gonji, horrified, remarks: 'You make it worse when you smile!'

The tonal shifts in *Yojimbo* are facilitated and accentuated by changes in Masaru Sato's excellent score. The theme accompanying Sanjuro's march into town is skilfully written, and perfectly conveys the energy and menace of his character.

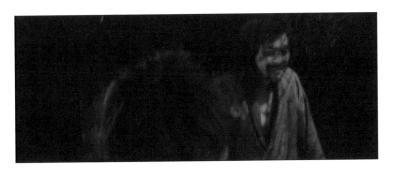

'You make it worse when you smile!' Sanjuro (Toshiro Mifune) tries his best to look healthy. *Yojimbo* directed by Akira Kurosawa and produced by Ryuzo Kikushima, Tomoyuki Tanaka and Akira Kurosawa for Toho Studios.

The entire cast of *Yojimbo* performs admirably but, as usual, special mention must go to Toshiro Mifune. Here he plays a character very different to his usual role of the loud, unkempt individual (for example, see his performances in *Seven Samurai*, *Red Lion* and *Daredevil in the Castle*), instead playing a stern ronin with a streak of dark humour. Also worthy of mention is Tatsuya Nakadai, who performs admirably as the sadistic Unosuke, foreshadowing his classic portrayal of Ryunosuke in *Sword of Doom*.

Japanese audiences appreciated the innovations in Kurosawa's film, and both *Yojimbo* and its sequel, *Sanjuro*, were hugely successful. This success was so widespread that many other samurai film directors adopted their sombre tone and graphic portrayal of violence, which led to huge changes in the genre.

Yojimbo also had a considerable effect on how the anti-hero was represented, both in samurai films and genres outside of Japanese cinema. Sanjuro is clearly an individual of high morals. He cleans up the town because he finds corruption there; he doesn't profit from this course of action, and, in fact, nearly dies. Coupled with Sanjuro's morality, however, is a callous disregard for the lives of those he judges to be evil, which clearly places him in the category of anti-hero. While

Kurosawa is not the first to use the anti-hero in a genre film, in *Yojimbo* he creates his own unique brand of anti-heroism.

Yojimbo was remade by an Italian, Sergio Leone, as *A Fistful of Dollars*, a hugely successful film which was the first of the spaghetti western genre. Leone's adaptation of *Yojimbo* was completely unauthorised, something which understandably frustrated Kurosawa. He took legal action against Leone, in which he was successful, and was awarded a percentage of the takings of *A Fistful of Dollars*.

Leone's central character, played by Clint Eastwood, also displayed a black comedy in his callousness, and was even more of an anti-hero than Sanjuro; Leone's gunslinger takes on the gangs for no reason other than profit, and at the end of the film walks away with hundreds of dollars, unlike Sanjuro, who leaves only with his life and his sword. This cool form of anti-heroism would persist through the entire spaghetti western genre, which in turn would have a large effect on genre films worldwide.

THE VERDICT

Every aspect of *Yojimbo* shines; Kurosawa creates a highly evocative tone, at times both deliciously sombre and hilariously funny. This combined with vigorous performances from Toshiro Mifune and Tatsuya Nakadai creates what is not only one of the greatest samurai films of all time, but also one of the most entertaining films of any genre. This is the perfect place to start if you haven't seen any samurai films.

Sanjuro (1962)

Japanese Title: *Tsubaki Sanjuro*
Directed by: Akira Kurosawa
Written by: Adapted by Ryuzo Kikushima, Hideo Oguni and Akira Kurosawa from the novel by Shugoro Yamamoto
Produced by: Ryuzo Kikushima, Tomoyuki Tanaka
Edited by: Akira Kurosawa

Cinematography: Fukuzo Koizumi, Takao Saito
Cast: Toshiro Mifune (Sanjuro), Tatsuya Nakadai (Hanbei), Yuzo Kayama (Iori), Reiko Dan (Chidori), Takashi Shimura (Kurofuji), Kamatari Fujiwara (Takebayashi), Takako Irie (Mutsuta's wife), Masao Shimizu (Kikui), Yunosuke Ito (Mutsuta)

PLOT SUMMARY

Overhearing a group of young samurai plotting to find and remove corrupt officials in their clan, Sanjuro, the ronin we met in *Yojimbo*, reluctantly offers them his advice and help. Sanjuro deduces that Chamberlain Mutsuta, the man the youths suspect, is, in fact, a good man, and that Superintendent Kikui, the man the youths thought was their ally, is actually the leader of the conspiracy. Sanjuro saves the youths from the conspirator's men, then sets about helping them free the Chamberlain, who has been captured by Kikui and his men, who are attempting to make him sign a false confession. Sanjuro gains the trust of Hanbei, one of the leading samurai amongst the conspirators, and infiltrates their group. Although exposed as a traitor by Hanbei, Sanjuro is able to send his troops on a false errand, creating an opportunity for the youths to capture the ringleaders and rescue the Chamberlain, which they do. Sanjuro turns down a place in the clan, a reward offered for his efforts, and finds Hanbei waiting for him. In a final duel Sanjuro is victorious, but counsels the youths against becoming killers.

ANALYSIS

Sanjuro is Kurosawa's sequel to *Yojimbo*, and was just as much a commercial success. Toshiro Mifune reprises his role as Sanjuro, the wandering ronin, and brings the same cynicism and harsh sense of humour to the character as he did in *Yojimbo*. This time Sanjuro becomes embroiled in an internal dispute taking place in a large samurai clan.

Like *Yojimbo*, *Sanjuro* manages to be both brutal and humorous. Much of the humour comes from Sanjuro's interaction with the young samurai, who for all their righteous zeal are woefully ineffective in the cunning game of wits Sanjuro must undertake against the corrupt officials. The youths' constant blundering, and Sanjuro's reaction, creates the opportunity for several comic set pieces, all of which work extremely well thanks to a clever script and perfect comic timing from the well-picked cast. In one scene, Sanjuro is finally able to convince the young samurai that the best course of action is to wait and see what move their enemy makes. The youths rush around excitedly (and ineffectually), while the poor, exhausted ronin tries to get some sleep. This soon becomes impossible, as the youths constantly slam the door, waking Sanjuro each time he nods off.

The battle scenes in *Sanjuro* actually manage to exceed the violence of *Yojimbo*, quite an achievement in early 1960s Japan. Sanjuro's altercation with a large group of armed warriors at the film's beginning is greatly enhanced by the added sound effect of his sword cutting through fabric and flesh. The duel at *Sanjuro*'s conclusion is a true milestone for the samurai film, being the first to use the spraying-blood special effect which has become a staple of the genre. To achieve the effect fake blood is held under pressure and then released at the appropriate moment, creating a vibrant spray of blood as a character is cut down. It is surely here that it is used to its greatest effect. As in *Yojimbo*, the violence in *Sanjuro* is often surprising, and used with great economy to punctuate key moments of the film.

Kurosawa flawlessly balances the humorous and violent aspects of his film, creating a highly entertaining product. However, *Sanjuro* is also thought-provoking, and for all its graphic fight sequences, ultimately delivers a condemnation of violence. Unlike *Yojimbo*, in *Sanjuro*, the callous ronin actually meets someone who he can learn from. After rescuing the Chamberlain's wife, Sanjuro is forced to consider his actions more carefully when she admonishes him for killing too readily. She likens Sanjuro to a sword, saying he is too sharp. Sanjuro is forced to yield to her wisdom, later becoming enraged when the blundering of the young samurai forces him to kill some of the conspirator's men. Sanjuro is presented at the end of the film as a slightly tragic character; he doesn't want to kill but frequently finds it necessary for his survival. He is offered a place in the clan, but cannot accept because he's accustomed to the freedom of his ronin lifestyle; he has no place in civilised society. Kurosawa presents the anti-violent message in his film through a series of clever lines and Sanjuro's predicament. This message is integrated seamlessly into the film, and loses none of its integrity.

THE VERDICT

Like *Yojimbo*, *Sanjuro* is an absolute classic, and a must-see for anyone interested in samurai films, featuring swift battle scenes, humorous and well-crafted characters and a thought-provoking plot.

The Tale of Zatoichi (1962)

Japanese Title: *Zatoichi monogatari*
Directed by: Kenji Misumi
Written by: Adapted by Minoru Inuzuka from a story by Kan Shimozawa
Produced by: Ikuo Kubodera
Edited by: Kanji Suganuma
Cinematography: Chishi Makiura
Cast: Shintaro Katsu (Zatoichi), Masayo Banri (Tane), Michio Minami (Tate), Shigeru Amachi (Hirate), Eijiro Yanagi (Sukegoro), Ryuzo Shimada (Shigezo), Hajime Mitamura (Hanji), Manabu Morita (Seisuke)

PLOT SUMMARY

Zatoichi, the blind masseur and deadly swordsman, arrives in the town of Iioka. He decides to stay with Sukegoro, a yakuza boss he knows. Sukegoro is preparing for a war with his rival, Shigezo. He hopes to use

Zatoichi's skill on his side, and does all he can to keep the blind man happy, assigning Tate, one of his nastier thugs, to look after him. Zatoichi spends his time in Iioka relaxing, fishing at a nearby lake, where he meets Hirate, a disgraced samurai hired by Shigezo. The two form a strong friendship, realising they may face each other on the battlefield. Zatoichi rescues Tane, Tate's sister, from Seisuke, a yakuza thug who desires her, and she falls in love with him. The tensions between the two gangs escalate and result in a war. It seems as though both Zatoichi and Hirate won't participate, but Hirate is manipulated into fighting by Shigezo, which also draws Zatoichi into the fray. Hirate insists they fight, as he wants to die at the hands of a master, rather than thugs. Zatoichi wins the duel, but is sad to have lost his friend. Sukegoro's men win the battle, and Zatoichi yells at him for the pointless waste of so many men, before seeing to Hirate's burial. Tate attempts to kill him, but only ends up killing himself. Tane waits on the road for Zatoichi but he avoids her by taking a longer route through the mountains.

ANALYSIS

The Tale of Zatoichi is the first film in the immensely popular Zatoichi series, which tells the story of the highly skilled blind swordsman. This first entry is atypical of the series, which is most famous for frequent and well-executed battle scenes in which Zatoichi cuts down large groups of his enemies. *The Tale of Zatoichi* takes a more gentle and thoughtful approach to deliver its character-driven story.

Interestingly, the Zatoichi series begins with a film that's much closer to the work of Akira Kurosawa and Hiroshi Inagaki. Director Kenji Misumi delivers some poignant scenes, both beautiful and revealing. In the best of these Zatoichi and Hirate sit at the riverbank fishing; Misumi creates a sense of tranquillity with shots of the two warriors sitting in the sun, intermixed with shots of the still water, disturbed only by their fishing lines. Misumi reveals much about the two characters during this scene. Special mention must be made of the way he handles Zatoichi's amazing abilities, which require more than a little suspension of disbelief. As Hirate approaches Zatoichi, who sits fishing, Misumi uses a simple technique to show how the blind swordsman's other senses compensate for his lack of sight. Close-ups of Hirate's feet falling on the grass are intermixed with close-ups of Zatoichi's ear, the sound of Hirate's feet playing across both these shots. This technique is repeated with a shot of Hirate's sword, which Zatoichi can hear moving in his belt. This sequence makes later scenes, such as the moment when Zatoichi cuts a lit candle perfectly in half, all the more believable.

Minoru Inuzuka creates some beautifully poetic moments in his script, which revolve around Zatoichi's blindness. When he rescues Tane from the lustful Seisuke, Zatoichi pretends he doesn't know Seisuke is present. Then, as he leads Tane away, Zatoichi dares Seisuke to attack him, asking if anyone is indeed there. Seisuke is afraid and cowers away, and Zatoichi laughs, seeming to chide himself for the mistake, when in reality he knows exactly what has happened. A similar moment occurs at the end of the film, achieved through Inuzuka's clever dialogue – but to say more would ruin the moment for anyone who hasn't seen it.

As always, Shintaro Katsu puts in a great performance as Zatoichi. He's more restrained here than in later films, but still presents a very likeable, affable hero. The kindness and warmth of Katsu's Zatoichi has endeared him to fans all over the world.

Though there are fewer of them, *The Tale of Zatoichi* still mounts some very well-choreographed battle scenes. When Zatoichi slices a lit candle clean in half, his blade moves so fast it's barely visible. During the sequences in which yakuza gangs fight, a slow pan effectively captures a mass of writhing bodies and flashing blades. A few wonderfully gory moments are scattered throughout the film, most notably when Hirate vomits blood all over his feet. The duel between Zatoichi and Hirate towards the end of the film is particularly adept at conveying the dramatic weight of what has happened. Katsu convincingly portrays Zatoichi's sadness for having killed his friend, provoking a profound sense of loss.

Shintaro Katsu as Zatoichi. *The Tale of Zatoichi* directed by Kenji Misumi and produced by Ikuo Kubodera for Daiei Studios.

THE VERDICT

Atypical of the popular series it spawned, *The Tale of Zatoichi* is still a solid film, and a must-see for anyone interested in Zatoichi's humble beginnings.

The Tale of Zatoichi Continues (1962)

Japanese Title: *Zoku Zatoichi monogatari*
Directed by: Kazuo Mori
Written by: Adapted by Minoru Inuzuka from a story by Kan Shimozawa
Produced by: Ikuo Kubodera
Edited by: Koji Taniguchi
Cinematography: Shozo Honda
Cast: Shintaro Katsu (Zatoichi), Yoshie Mizutani (Setsu), Masayo Banri (Tane), Tomisaburo Wakayama – credited as Kenzaburo Jo – (Yoshiro), Yutaka Nakamura (Sanzo), Sonosuke Sawamura (Kanbei), Eijiro Yanagi (Sukegoro)

PLOT SUMMARY

Zatoichi makes an enemy of the Kuroda clan, but Setsu, a woman who reminds him of his first love, Chiyo, helps him to escape them. Unable to find Zatoichi, the Kuroda samurai hire Kanbei, the local yakuza boss, to track him down. Zatoichi escapes Kanbei's men, and returns to Sasagawa, where he plans to pay his respects to Hirate (see *Tale of Zatoichi*). Kanbei and his men pursue Zatoichi, and meet with Sukegoro, who agrees to help them. Sukegoro has also been harbouring Yoshiro, a wanted criminal. Sukegoro tells him to leave immediately, but has him followed, planning to betray Yoshiro to the authorities and collect a large reward. Kanbei and his men confront Zatoichi and a violent battle ensues. In an impressive display of swordsmanship, Zatoichi kills all the men, leaving only Kanbei alive. Yoshiro appears and challenges Zatoichi. It turns out that the two are brothers; Chiyo left Zatoichi when she discovered he was blind and married Yoshiro. In his rage, Zatoichi cut Yoshiro's arm off. Yoshiro now wants to settle the score and nearly succeeds, but Zatoichi is able to deal him a serious wound. Sukegoro and his men arrive, intent on capturing Yoshiro. Zatoichi helps Yoshiro escape, but he dies from his wounds. Zatoichi is enraged. Finding Sukegoro, Zatoichi kills him for betraying his brother.

ANALYSIS

A satisfying sequel to *Tale of Zatoichi*, this pushed the series forward with the kind of film that would come to dominate the series. Around 20 minutes shorter than the first, *The Tale of Zatoichi Continues* packs in a lot more of the frenetic fight scenes that would become a hallmark of the Zatoichi films.

And what magnificent fight scenes they are. The sight of Shintaro Katsu cleaving his way through a large number of yakuza thugs is a delight to behold. Although it may seem hard to believe that a man could fight so effectively without being able to see, Katsu's astonishingly convincing movements make it easy to suspend disbelief. He fights with his head bowed low, clearly concentrating on every sound around him, and strikes only when his opponents move.

Katsu's performance as Zatoichi is as likeable as ever, but in this film his affable persona is offset by his creepy brother Yoshiro, played by Katsu's real brother, Tomisaburo Wakayama. As Yoshiro, Wakayama plays a grim and inexpressive man of few words, who murders only for the sake of money. Wakayama's cold stare is every bit as frightening as Katsu's chuckle is friendly, and his performance pre-dates his later role as Ogami Itto in the *Lone Wolf and Cub* series.

Director Kazuo Mori handles the highly charged fight scenes very well. Yet, there are some touching moments between the bloody scenes, which hark back to *Tale of Zatoichi*. Zatoichi's brief experience of domesticity with the beautiful Setsu is tender, and made all the more fleeting by the arrival of Kanbei's thugs. The moment when Zatoichi returns to the lake where he and Hirate used to go fishing, and considers his life thus far, is suitably calm. The moment when Yoshiro dies, just after the two brothers have ended their long feud, is emotionally charged and sensitively handled.

THE VERDICT

With this film, the Zatoichi series found the voice it would use for the next 24 films. Some Zatoichi films contain even more action, but *The Tale of Zatoichi Continues* founded its reputation for well-executed, and bloody, battle scenes. Essential for Zatoichi fans, this film is worth seeing alone for Katsu and Wakayama's performances.

The 47 Ronin (1962)

Japanese Title: *Chushingura – Hana no maki yuki no maki*
Directed by: Hiroshi Inagaki
Written by: Adapted by Toshio Yasumi from the play by Shoraku

Miyoshi, Senryu Namiki, Izumo Takeda

Produced by: Sanezumi Fujimoto, Tomoyuki Tanaka, Hiroshi Inagaki

Edited by: Hirokazu Iwashita

Cinematography: Kazuo Yamada

Cast: Koshiro Matsumoto (Chamberlain Kuranosuke Oishi), Yuzo Kayama (Lord Naganori Asano), Chusha Ichikawa (Lord Yoshinaga Kira), Tatsuya Mihashi (Yasubei Horibe), Akira Takarada (Gunpei Takada), Yosuke Natsuki (Kinemon Okano), Makoto Sato (Kazuemon Fuwa), Tadao Takashima (Jyujiro Kan), Takashi Shimura (Hyuobu Chishaka), Toshiro Mifune (Genba Tawaraboshi), Setsuko Hara (Riku Oishi), Yuriko Hoshi (Otsuya)

PLOT SUMMARY

When Lord Asano is appointed Head of Reception for an important cere-mony, he refuses to bribe Kira, the Grand Master of Ceremonies, a particularly nasty, greedy old man. Despite Kira's bullying, Asano won't break from his principles. The strain grows too much for Asano when Kira refuses to tell him how to conduct the ceremony, and he draws his sword, trying to cut down his tormentor. Having drawn his sword in the Shogun's palace, Asano is sentenced to commit seppuku. Asano's samurai are displeased, and wish to remain in Asano's castle and fight the troops sent to claim it. Oishi, the Chamberlain of the Asano samurai, convinces them to leave peacefully, hoping to reinstate the clan with Daigaku, Asano's brother, as the new lord. When the Shogun banishes Daigaku, Oishi is forced to reconsider his position. He decides on a course of justice, seeking to punish Kira for his crimes. Oishi lives a false life, as a decadent drunk, hoping to fool Kira and his allies. Many of the other ronin make similar sacrifices. They are successful in fooling the authorities, and when the time comes, they assemble in Edo. In a brave assault on Kira's mansion, the 47 ronin find and behead him. The ronin are then ordered to commit seppuku, a punishment they accept, now that they've found justice for their dead lord.

ANALYSIS

The 47 Ronin is a true classic of the samurai film genre, and captures the very essence of the samurai ideal. Based on historical events, which have become legendary through numerous retellings, *The 47 Ronin* is a story of total loyalty and dedication.

The story of the 47 loyal ronin is a traditional tale in Japan, and one which Japanese audiences in 1962 would have been very familiar with, in much the same way that archetypical stories such as *Romeo and Juliet* are immediately recognisable to western audiences. As such, *The 47 Ronin* can be a bit confusing to those unfamiliar with the traditional stories. There are lots of characters and subplots, all variously linked to the central story of the ronin. Don't be at all surprised if you find it difficult to remember who certain characters are; many are only introduced very briefly. This is not a fault in the film; Japanese audiences would have no problem following the story, simply because they already know it. Don't be too concerned about following the various subplots first time round; the central story is the most important, and is a rewarding viewing experience all of its own. With subsequent viewings, the subplots become easier to follow, and make *The 47 Ronin* an even more enriching film.

Having said this, the film's basic plot is a moving experience, and shows the best side of the samurai's dedication and loyalty. The hardships the ronin suffer, and the sacrifices they are prepared to make, all for the sake of their dead lord, are truly amazing, and make for compelling viewing. Chamberlain Oishi makes the biggest sacrifice of all: in order to fool his enemies, Oishi divorces his wife and adopts the life of a lazy playboy, much to the scorn and ridicule of many other ronin. It's particularly moving when Oishi hears of the death of one of the ronin; struggling to contain his emotions he continues to party in a brothel, sad that his friend has died, but unable to show it. Another of the ronin, Okano, makes a similarly difficult sacrifice: he courts Otsuya, the sister of a carpenter, in order to get the plans to Kira's new house. When Okano realises he actually loves the girl, he grows to despise himself for using her, but does so anyway, and secures the plans. The manner in which these men put aside all their personal concerns to pursue their just cause is a perfect representation of the unwavering loyalty of the ideal samurai.

Director Hiroshi Inagaki gives this story the epic treatment it deserves, taking us inside lush mansions and palaces, and, as always, making use of beautiful Japanese landscapes. Having already told the epic story of master swordsman Miyamoto Musashi, Inagaki has the right experience to make the best of such larger-than-life material. The battle at the end of the film is magnificent; the 47 ronin fight their way through Kira's mansion in a series of beautifully choreographed fight scenes, which not only look fantastic, but are also extremely convincing.

THE VERDICT

A classic film, although potentially confusing to non-Japanese audiences. Don't make this your first samurai film; Inagaki's *Samurai Trilogy* or Kurosawa's *Yojimbo* are much better places to start. However, if you like the genre, and want to see what bushido really meant, then make sure to watch *The 47 Ronin*.

Hara-kiri (1962)

Japanese Title: *Seppuku*
Directed by: Masaki Kobayashi
Written by: Story by Yasuhiko Takiguchi, screenplay by Shinobu Hashimoto
Produced by: Tatsuo Hosoya
Edited by: Hisashi Sagara
Cinematography: Yoshio Miyajima
Cast: Tatsuya Nakadai (Hanshiro), Rentaro Mikuni (Kageyu), Shima

Iwashita (Miho), Akira Ishihama (Motome), Tetsuro Tamba (Hikokuro), Yoshio Aoki (Umenosuke), Ichiro Nakaya (Hayato), Yoshio Inaba (Jinnai)

PLOT SUMMARY

In recent times many impoverished ronin have arrived at clan mansions, and requested to commit ritual suicide in their grounds, claiming that they can no longer endure their impoverished lifestyles. Yet most have no desire to kill themselves, knowing full well that the clans will give them money simply to be rid of them. This presents a problem for the clans, who see this as a form of extortion. When Motome, a young ronin, requests to commit suicide in the Iyi mansion, rather than simply deny the request or give him money, Kageyu, the clan counsellor, has his samurai force the young man to commit hara-kiri, even refusing his request for a two-day postponement. As if this isn't bad enough, they make him use the bamboo sword he carries; he is so poor he has sold his blades. This is all done to preserve the honour of the Iyi clan and deter other ronin. Motome had a sick child, and needed money for medicine – he was only driven to performing the hara-kiri scam by the most extreme circumstances.

The film revolves around Hanshiro, father-in-law of Motome. Himself a ronin, Hanshiro realises he is most happy when he has no superiors and is with his family. He praises his son-in-law for his brave actions, and curses his own stupidity for not selling his swords. Hanshiro exposes the hypocrisy of the Iyi by also requesting to commit hari-kiri within their castle grounds. He has previously removed the top knots of the three retainers most involved in Motome's enforced suicide. According to the samurai code this is a grave dishonour, and can only be atoned by hara-kiri. Hanshiro requests that these men assist with his suicide, but two of them hide in their homes, waiting for their hair to re-grow, demonstrating the same cowardice they accused Motome of. Kageyu has his men attack Hanshiro, and he fights bravely, eventually succumbing to the Iyi's guns. With Hanshiro dead, Kageyu sets about concealing the entire incident, something he does so well that the Iyi clan is praised for its handling of the ronin.

ANALYSIS

Hara-kiri is a tremendous film, and among the most moving and honest of the samurai genre. Director Masaki Kobayashi, famous for films which explored the downtrodden, makes clear here the potential for the inhumane cruelty inherent in the samurai code. This is in stark contrast to many other samurai films, which portray the harsh lifestyle of the samurai in a positive light.

Kobayashi shows the propensity of the samurai for senseless cruelty through the actions of the Iyi clan. Their inhuman treatment of Motome is done entirely to preserve the good name of their clan, and this, in essence, is the fault in the samurai philosophy that Kobayashi is drawing our attention to; reputation should never be a justification for cruelty, and is far less important than the ethical treatment of human beings. This is also highlighted through the character of Hanshiro, who comes to realise that those he loves are far more important than the social standing he has lost.

The story of Hanshiro and Motome is moving, and the audience cannot help but feel for their plight. Yet, Kageyu and the Iyi learn nothing from these sad events; the hiding retainers are also forced to commit hara-kiri, and the entire incident is concealed in the clan records. The Iyi are even praised for the way they dealt with the situation. This shows the stubborn and unbending nature of the samurai code, which ultimately only history was able to defeat.

This frank and unyielding plot is effectively rendered by Kobayashi's skilled direction, and some robust performances. The film abounds with memorable scenes and images. The scene in which Motome is forced to cut his stomach open with a bamboo blade is harrowing in its brutality; we see Motome trying to force the blunt object into his chest many times, finally succeeding when he puts his full weight on it. Akira

Ishihama convincingly conveys the agony and desperation, which in its gory explicitness conveys the cruelty of the Iyi samurai. The battle between Hanshiro and the Iyi samurai is very well realised, and more realistically than in many other samurai films. It is clear that Hanshiro won't survive against so many enemies, and he becomes progressively more injured and fatigued as the battle progresses. His duel with Hikokuro is also of the highest quality, filmed in long grass on a windy day with the constantly shifting grass creating a moody backdrop. Many highly evocative and symbolic single frames pepper *Hara-kiri*, such as the large Iyi clan crest, splattered in blood during Hanshiro's battle with the Iyi samurai.

Tatsuya Nakadai delivers one of his best performances as Hanshiro, and skilfully shows a wide range of emotions. We see Hanshiro at several different stages of his life, and Nakadai presents them all with complete conviction. The sensitivity of Nakadai's performance imbues the scenes where he happily plays with his grandson with a touching quality, and makes the events which befall his family all the more tragic. In contrast, Nakadai's portrayal of the later Hanshiro, who, having lost everything, is disturbingly morose and inexpressive, creates a character that's both sympathetic and slightly disturbing. Nakadai's performance in

Hanshiro (Tatsuya Nakadai) battles the Iyi samurai. *Hara-kiri* directed by Masaki Kobayashi and produced by Tatsuo Hosoya for Shochiku Studios.

this film is rightly hailed by many as one of the greatest of the samurai film genre.

THE VERDICT

The stark honesty of *Hara-kiri* exposes a side of the samurai code ignored by many other samurai films. With a moving plot, a classic performance by Tatsuya Nakadai and assured direction by Masaki Kobayashi, it's a captivating film. Not only for samurai film fans, *Hara-kiri* is an example of cinema at its best.

New Tale of Zatoichi (1963)

Japanese Title: *Shin Zatoichi monogatari*
Directed by: Tokuzo Tanaka
Written by: Adapted by Minoru Inozuka from a story by Kan Shimozawa
Produced by: Masaichi Nagata
Edited by: Hiroshi Yamada
Cinematography: Chishi Makiura
Cast: Shintaro Katsu (Zatoichi), Mikiko Tsubouchi, Chitose Maki, Mieko Kondo, Seizaburo Kawazu

PLOT SUMMARY

Zatoichi, the blind master swordsman, grows tired of his violent lifestyle, and resolves to lead a peaceful life. He meets with Banno, the ronin who taught him swordsmanship, and stays in his village for some time. Banno is a respected teacher, but he is secretly involved with the Tengu group, a gang of fugitive ronin. His main concern, however, is ensuring that his sister, Yoyoi, marries into a rich family so he can regain a little of his lost status. Banno and the Tengu gang hatch a plot to kidnap one of his students, who has a wealthy father. They are successful and arrange to collect the ransom. Zatoichi and Yoyoi's relationship develops, and the two wish to marry. They ask Banno's permission, but he flies into a rage, refusing to let Yoyoi marry someone of such low status. Humiliated, Zatoichi leaves. He also discovers Banno's plot. The next morning, the Tengu group set out to collect their ransom. They are intercepted by Zatoichi who kills them all. Banno, meanwhile, kills the father of his pupil, stealing the ransom money, which he plans to use to buy a lavish wedding for Yoyoi. Zatoichi confronts Banno and narrowly defeats him in a tense battle, witnessed by Yoyoi. Realising that he will never escape violence, Zatoichi continues his nomadic lifestyle, leaving Yoyoi behind.

ANALYSIS

New Tale of Zatoichi, the third entry in the Zatoichi series, is an involving film that brings a new dimension to the blind swordsman. In this sad tale, Zatoichi is forced to consider the morality of his lifestyle, a lifestyle he is ultimately unable to escape.

The film's production values are much higher than the first two. Clearly Daiei were prepared to spend a lot more on this film, based on the success of previous Zatoichi episodes. *New Tale of Zatoichi* benefits from vibrant colours and smooth pans, and, in many ways, heralded the quality production values, emotional stories and large helpings of yakuza carnage that the series would go on to deliver.

These improved production values bring to life a script of a high standard, which in turn is supported by Shintaro Katsu's emotive performance. It is Zatoichi's attempt to change his violent lifestyle which is the most compelling and dramatic aspect of Kan Shimozawa and Minoru Inozuka's story. Katsu has no trouble grasping these new elements of Zatoichi's character. He portrays the blind swordsman's hopes for a non-violent lifestyle, his joy when he thinks he has found it, and his anger and sadness when it is taken away from him, with such conviction and integrity that only the hardest of viewers could fail to be touched by his plight. The scenes between Zatoichi and Yoyoi are played at just the right dramatic level to elicit audience sympathy.

Like *The Tale of Zatoichi Continues*, *New Tale of Zatoichi* contains a plethora of terrific fight scenes. Katsu is at his sword-swinging best, this time fighting not only yakuza, but a nasty group of itinerant ronin, the Tengu group. The duel at the film's conclusion between Zatoichi and Banno is swift and unpredictable, creating an evocative atmosphere; for a few tense moments it's impossible to know who has won.

THE VERDICT

The Zatoichi series just gets better and better. With the third film, the series was really getting into its stride, presenting a likeable, morally conflicted hero, and a host of wonderfully executed fight scenes. *New Tale of Zatoichi* is a great way to introduce yourself to the series (there's no need to have seen the first two films) and it's a good representation of the series as a whole. A real treat for those interested in Zatoichi and samurai films in general.

Three Outlaw Samurai (1964)

Japanese Title: *Sanbiki no samurai*
Directed by: Hideo Gosha
Written by: Keiichi Abe, Eizaburo Shiba, Hideo Gosha
Produced by: Ginichi Kishimoto, Tetsuro Tamba
Edited by: Kazuo Ota
Cinematography by: Tadashi Sakai
Cast: Tetsuro Tamba (Shiba), Mikijiro Hira (Kikyo), Isamu Nagato (Sakura), Miyuki Kuwano (Aya), Kamatari Fujiwara (Jinbei), Yoko Mihara (Maki), Toshie Kimura (Ine), Tatsuya Ishiguro (Matsushita), Yoshiko Kayama (Oyasu), Jun Tatara (Yasugoro), Kyoko Aoi (Mitsu)

PLOT SUMMARY

Shiba, a wandering ronin, helps some peasants who are being overtaxed by their cruel magistrate. Jinbei, the leader of the peasants, has captured Aya, the magistrate's daughter, and hopes to exchange her for a reduction in taxes. Shiba helps the peasants against the magistrate and his men, who attack the old mill where Aya is held. Sakura, a ronin sent by the magistrate, decides to join the peasant side. The hostage situation is finally broken when some ronin hired by the magistrate kidnap Yasu, the daughter of Gasaku, one of the peasants in the mill. Although Yasu kills herself, hoping that her father won't give in, Shiba and the others are drawn out of the mill, and Aya is returned to her father. Shiba strikes a bargain with the magistrate, accepting punishment for the peasants' crimes: 100 lashes, on the condition that there are no other retributions. The magistrate does not keep his word: he tortures Shiba and has three of the peasants killed by his ronin. Kikyo, one of the magistrate's samurai, disapproves of his treachery and helps Sakura and Aya, who has grown to love Shiba, free him. The magistrate sends some of his samurai after Kikyo, and this forces him to join Shiba's side. Shiba and Kikyo have a showdown with the most skilled swordsmen in the magistrate's clan. Although bribed to leave by the magistrate, Sakura arrives to help his friends, and they are victorious. Despite his best efforts, Shiba cannot convince the terrified peasants to take their complaints to the magistrate's daimyo. Enraged, he goes to kill the magistrate, but is stopped by Aya's pleading for his life. The three outlaws leave, travelling the road together.

ANALYSIS

Three Outlaw Samurai is the first film of Hideo Gosha, a talented director who would go on to make many memorable samurai films. It's actually adapted from a TV series that Gosha directed, and he shows his considerable talent for cinema in his first feature-length project.

Gosha's primary concern here is telling an exciting and entertaining story, and he draws on his earlier experience as a director for television to well and truly deliver. As Patrick Galloway has pointed out, Gosha's

TV-style direction imbues his films with a fast, rhythmic pace and a sense of immediacy that clearly sets him apart from other samurai film directors. Gosha tends not to use static scenic shots, like Kurosawa and Inagaki did to great effect throughout their careers, but instead relies on a rapid progression of lively scenes. This pacing and rhythm imbues Gosha's films with a life of their own, giving the impression of a story that's constantly in motion.

The plot of the film is one of its finest strengths. A fairly simple tale about three ronin helping peasants against a cruel magistrate, the plot has clearly defined good guys and bad guys, yet pits them against each other in interesting ways. The hostage situation at the beginning of the film, and the horrible way it's ultimately resolved, makes for compelling viewing, as do the scenes in which the ronin and the peasants are confronted by the magistrate's brutal, hired thugs.

Three Outlaw Samurai shares some similarities in both tone and plot with Kurosawa's immensely successful *Yojimbo* and *Sanjuro*. Indeed, as both Alain Silver and Patrick Galloway have pointed out, Gosha likes to quote these and other films in his work. However, rather than try to copy the darkly comedic tone of these films, Gosha creates a different, though no less satisfying, feeling. His characters are not such extreme anti-heroes as Sanjuro, because they are not as callous about the loss of human life. Shiba helps the peasants out of a desire to prevent blood-shed, rather than a wish to inflict it on evil men, which is one of Sanjuro's motivations in *Yojimbo*. Similarly, it is hard to imagine Sanjuro showing the mercy Shiba does at the end of the film, or being as guilty about a single death as Sakura is. In many respects, this makes Gosha's heroes much easier to relate to than Kurosawa's anti-heroes. Rather than the dark comedy that's employed by Kurosawa, Gosha creates a tone of camaraderie between his three, very likeable central characters, which extends to the audience.

These three central heroes are very well cast. Tetsuro Tamba, with his chiselled jaw and stern delivery, is perfect as the morally heroic Shiba, a man who sticks to his principles no matter what. Isamu Nagato plays the

The three outlaws: Shiba (Tetsuro Tamba), Kikyo (Mikijiro Hira) and Sakura (Isamu Nagato). *Three Outlaw Samurai* directed by Hideo Gosha and produced by Ginichi Kishimoto and Tetsuro Tamba for Shochiku Studios.

slightly more flawed, and thus comic, Sakura, who not only provides occasional humour but also drama. Mikijiro Hira is the slightly ambiguous Kikyo; with just the right amount of inscrutability, we're unsure which side he will ultimately take right up to the point he actually makes his decision. These three central characters, the three outlaws of the title, are the driving force behind Gosha's film and the end result is a credit both to the script and their talent.

Gosha shows right from the beginning that he has a great aptitude for directing battle scenes. Like the rest of the film, these fights have a wonderful sense of rhythm and pacing, yet never seem overly stylised. The film's finale, in which the three heroes do battle with skilled warriors from the magistrate's clan, is beautifully constructed, and Tamba, Nagato and Hira prove to be every bit as fun to watch cleaving through their enemies as Shintaro Katsu or Toshiro Mifune. Nagato is particularly entertaining as Sakura, enthusiastically swinging a spear rather than a sword.

A promotional poster for *Seven Samurai*. *Seven Samurai* directed by Akira Kurosawa and produced by Sojiro Motoki for Toho Studios. Image provided by Toho Company Ltd. and Photofest. © Toho Company Ltd.

Takezo (Toshiro Mifune) is only interested in perfecting his swordsmanship. *Miyamoto Musashi* directed by Hiroshi Inagaki and produced by Kazuo Takimura for Toho Studios.

Musashi (Toshiro Mifune) and Kojiro (Koji Tsuruta) during their epic duel. *Duel on Ganryu Island* directed by Hiroshi Inagaki and produced by Kazuo Takimura for Toho Studios.

Two icons of the samurai film finally meet in combat: the Yojimbo (Toshiro Mifune) and Zatoichi (Shintaro Katsu). *Zatoichi Meets Yojimbo* directed by Kihachi Okamoto and produced by Shintaro Katsu and Hiroyoshi Nishioka for Toho Studios.

o Ogami (Tomisaburo Wakayama), Daigoro (Akihiro Tomikawa) and their deadly baby cart. *Lone Wolf d Cub: Baby Cart on the River Styx* directed by Kenji Misumi and produced by Shintaro Katsu and saharu Matsubara for Toho Studios.

ki (Meiko Kaji) is an instrument of vengeance. *Lady Snowblood* directed by Toshiya Fujita and oduced by Kikumaru Okuda for Toho Studios.

A promotional poster for *Kagemusha*. *Kagemusha* directed by Akira Kurosawa and produced by Aki Kurosawa, Tomoyuki Tanaka, Francis Ford Coppola and George Lucas for Kurosawa Production Co., Tol Studios and 20th Century Fox. Image provided by 20th Century Fox and Photofest. © 20th Century Fc

Tatsuya Nakadai as Hidetora. *Ran* directed by Akira Kurosawa and produced by Katsumi Furukaw Masato Hara, Hisao Kurosawa and Serge Silberman for Greenwich Film Productions, Herald Ace Ir and Nippon Herald Films.

...o's army on the move. This beautiful image from *Ran* gives a good impression of the film's large-scale ...ttle scenes. *Ran* directed by Akira Kurosawa and produced by Katsumi Furukawa, Masato Hara, Hisao ...rosawa and Serge Silberman for Greenwich Film Productions, Herald Ace Inc. and Nippon Herald ...ms. Image provided by Orion Classics and Photofest. © Orion Classics.

...eibei (Hiroyuki Sanada) is both a caring father... *The Twilight Samurai* directed by Yoji Yamada and ...roduced by Hiroshi Fukazawa, Shigehiro Nakagawa and Ichiro Yamamoto for Hakuhodo, Nippon ...elevision Network Corporation and the Sumitomo Corporation.

...and a skilled warrior. *The Twilight Samurai* directed by Yoji Yamada and produced by Hiros▮ Fukazawa, Shigehiro Nakagawa, and Ichiro Yamamoto for Hakuhodo, Nippon Television Netwo▮ Corporation and the Sumitomo Corporation.

Takeshi Kitano as Zatoichi. *Zatoichi* (2003) directed by Takeshi Kitano and produced by Masayuki Mo▮ and Tsunehisa Saito for Bandai Visual Co., Saito Entertainment and Office Kitano Productions.

danobu Asano as Hattori and Takeshi Kitano as Zatoichi. *Zatoichi* (2003) directed by Takeshi Kitano
d produced by Masayuki Mori and Tsunehisa Saito for Bandai Visual Co., Saito Entertainment and
ffice Kitano Productions. Image provided by Miramax and Photofest. © Miramax.

n unusual duel in an unusual temple. *Aragami* directed by Ryuhei Kitamura and produced by Yuuji
hida, Shinya Kawai and Haruo Umekawa for Napalm Films, Amuse, Micott and DUEL film partners.

Yukiyoshi Ozawa as Yaichiro and Masatoshi Nagase as Munezo. *The Hidden Blade* directed by Yo
Yamada and produced by Hiroshi Fukazawa for Shochiku Co. Image provided by Shochiku, Tartan an
Photofest. © Shochiku.

Masatoshi Nagase as Munezo and Takako Matsu as Kie. *The Hidden Blade* directed by Yoji Yamada an
produced by Hiroshi Fukazawa for Shochiku Co. Image provided by Shochiku, Tartan and Photofes
© Shochiku.

THE VERDICT

With this terrific first film, Gosha earned himself a place alongside the other masters of the samurai film. Essential viewing.

Samurai Assassin (1965)

Japanese Title: *Samurai*
Directed by: Kihachi Okamoto
Written by: Adapted by Shinobu Hashimoto from the novel by Jiromasa Gunji
Produced by: Tomoyuki Tanaka, Reiji Miwa, Toshiro Mifune
Edited by: Yoshitami Kuroiwa
Cinematography: Hiroshi Murai
Cast: Toshiro Mifune (Niiro), Keiju Kobayashi (Kurihara), Michiyo Aratama (Okiku), Yunosuke Ito (Kenmotsu), Eijiro Tono (Kisoya), Koshiro Matsumoto (Li Naosuke), Tatsuyoshi Ehara (Hayama)

PLOT SUMMARY

A group of samurai plan to assassinate Li Naosuke, a daimyo and Elder of the Shogunate. Known as the Mito Tengu group, these conspirators are made up of samurai from clans which came off badly in a power struggle against Li, which led to many of their comrades being executed. Thus far, Li has been able to avoid the Tengu group, who believe there's a traitor in their ranks and begin to observe two ronin in their group, Niiro and Kurihara. Niiro doesn't know who his parents are; his mother, a concubine, told him he was of samurai blood, but refused to name his father. Looked after by Kisoya, a wealthy merchant, Niiro was trained as a samurai, but became a ronin when his request to marry a princess was denied by her daimyo father. Enraged, Niiro abandoned his studies and began life as a ruffian, all the while dreaming of becoming a samurai. He joins the Mito Tengu in the hope that if he kills Li he will be employed by one of the clans that hates him. Kurihara turns out to have a connection to Li through his wife, and Niiro is ordered to kill him. Despite being good friends with Kurihara, Niiro kills him, and is then angered to discover that Kurihara was not the traitor at all. The Tengu group discover that Niiro's father is in fact Li, and they attempt to have him killed. Niiro survives and arrives the next morning to attack Li. In a violent battle, most of the Tengu group and Li's entourage are killed, but Niiro succeeds in beheading Li, unaware that he has killed his father.

ANALYSIS

Samurai Assassin is a film rich with irony, suspense and violence. Directed by Kihachi Okamoto, who also made the thoroughly entertaining *Sword of Doom* and *Kill!*, *Samurai Assassin* is without doubt a standout samurai film.

The rich vein of irony that runs through *Samurai Assassin* is by far the film's most distinguishing feature. If you've skipped the above plot summary hoping not to spoil the film, then I suggest you stop reading this analysis, and see *Samurai Assassin* as soon as you can. Unfortunately, it is impossible to discuss this film without referring to some of the revelations contained within the plot.

Niiro Tsuruchiyo is so desperate to become an employed samurai that he joins a group of conspirators, who seek to kill Li Naosuke, a daimyo who has earned the ire of several clans. Li turns out to be Niiro's father, who could potentially make him a samurai, but Niiro, ignorant of this and desperate to impress the other clans, brutally kills Li. Furthermore, Li is the only man holding the Shogunate government together; without him, it will collapse, taking with it the samurai class. Niiro is completely unaware of the self-destructive nature of his actions, and there is a delicious sense of irony to this plot, which stays with the viewer for some time after the film. The scene of Niiro triumphantly staggering along, with Li's head on the end of his sword, is not only disturbing, but also strangely satisfying, as it serves to cement the ironic tone of *Samurai*

Assassin. Like all good tragedies, we know how this film is going to end, and like many samurai films, *Samurai Assassin* doesn't take the easy road with a happy ending. As we are left with the image of Niiro with his father's head on the end of his sword, we can only wonder at what will happen to him when he discovers the truth of what he has done.

Okamoto's direction in *Samurai Assassin* is of the high standard that fans have come to expect of him, especially in the battle scenes. The epic and extremely gory battle at the end of the film has got to be one of the finest in the genre. It begins with rapidly cut shots of the conspirators preparing themselves for the arrival of Li's entourage. They perform fast actions, checking swords, shutting umbrellas and kicking their sandals off – creating an impression of tension and anticipation. Once the battle actually starts, Okamoto spares no blood. The screen is filled with flailing bodies, striking at each other any way they can, covered in their own blood and that of their enemies. This all takes place on a thick cover of snow, which is quickly stained a dark colour. Snow falling from the sky also obscures the audience's view, creating a sense of chaotic confusion, which is suitable for the frenetic scenes taking place. Niiro's beheading of Li is particularly gory, with blood literally filling the entire screen.

THE VERDICT

Samurai Assassin combines a richly ironic plot with one of the most well-constructed battle scenes in the entire genre. This and *Sword of Doom* are Okamoto at his best.

Sword of Doom (1966)

Japanese Title: *Dai-bosatsu toge*
Directed by: Kihachi Okamoto
Written by: Adapted by Shinobu Hashimoto from the novel by Kaizan Nakazato
Produced by: Sanezumi Fujimoto, Kaneharu Minamizato, Masayuki Sato

Edited by: Yoshitami Kuroiwa
Cinematography: Hiroshi Murai
Cast: Tatsuya Nakadai (Ryunosuke), Yuzo Kayama (Hyoma), Michio Aratama (Ohama), Toshiro Mifune (Toranosuke), Yoko Naito (Omatsu), Tadao Nakamaru (Isamu), Ichiro Nakaya (Bunnojo)

PLOT SUMMARY

Ryunosuke, a swordsman renowned for his skill, is begged to let his opponent win in an upcoming fencing match by the man's wife, Ohama. Ohama secures Ryunosuke's promise to spare her husband by sleeping with him. Ryunosuke, however, wins the match, and kills his opponent in doing so. Forced to leave the school, Ryunosuke takes Ohama with him for now her family have rejected her. Ryunosuke falls in with a group of treacherous samurai and commits more murders in his thirst for power. But he cannot escape the consequences of his actions; some relatives of his victims are stalking him: a skilled young samurai and a thief armed with a revolver. Driven mad by visions of people he has murdered, Ryunosuke goes on a rampage through an inn, and the film ends suddenly with him badly wounded and surrounded by hostile samurai.

ANALYSIS

Sword of Doom is hailed by many samurai film fans as one of the greatest examples of the genre, and with outstanding direction by Kihachi Okamoto, and a classic performance by Tatsuya Nakadai, this praise is well earned.

Violent and sombre in tone, Ryunosuke kills often, and usually only to indulge his sadistic personality. He's a largely unsympathetic central character, which sets the film apart from most others in the samurai genre.

In arguably his greatest role, Tatsuya Nakadai's performance is highly evocative; his mixture of cold, uncaring stares and the occasional manic

Tatsuya Nakadai as Ryunosuke. *Sword of Doom* directed by Kihachi Okamoto and produced by Sanezumi Fujimoto, Kaneharu Minamizato and Masayuki Sato for Toho Studios.

expression perfectly conveys Ryunosuke's sociopath tendencies. During his fight scenes, Ryunosuke is methodical, coldly cutting down his enemies, on occasion showing joy as he does so. Nakadai conveys this well and to disturbing effect.

Okamoto's direction surpasses even his own high standards. The battles are swiftly paced, and Okamoto holds nothing back in his depiction of graphic violence. Ryunosuke's battle on a forest path with some disgruntled samurai is a good example of Okamoto's skill at action scenes. Shots from a variety of different angles show Ryunosuke methodically working through his enemies, cutting them down one at a time. When there are no more enemies left, he stops moving and we see a close-up of his profile, a sadistic smile creeping onto his lips. A classic shot of the forest path, strewn with bodies, follows and we see Ryunosuke, standing motionless in the distance. In a later scene, Okamoto again makes use of snow, as he did in *Samurai Assassin*. When Toranosuke, a skilled samurai sternly played by Toshiro Mifune, is confronted by a violent group of samurai conspirators, he is forced to fight them on a snow-covered road. In a particularly violent moment, he cuts one of his enemies' hands off, which we see fall to the ground, and stain the snow.

Ryunosuke (Tatsuya Nakadai) follows the path of cruelty. *Sword of Doom* directed by Kihachi Okamoto and produced by Sanezumi Fujimoto, Kaneharu Minamizato and Masayuki Sato for Toho Studios.

The scenes in which Ryunosuke goes on a rampage through an inn are among the best ever shot in a samurai film. Believing the ghosts of those he has harmed are haunting him, he sees their looming, shadowy forms on the paper walls surrounding him, and hears them mocking him. Striking at these phantoms, Ryunosuke completely destroys the room. As he slashes through each wall, there is a sharp cry of pain, as if Ryunosuke believes he is really harming these imagined enemies, but they continue to taunt him. These scenes offer a disturbing insight into Ryunosuke's twisted mind, and lead to an incredibly violent battle scene, in which he's confronted by the samurai conspirators he is supposed to be a member of.

While Ryunosuke himself is an unsympathetic character, the victims of his violent actions form an emotional connection with the audience. We follow the fortunes of several such characters. Particularly tragic is Ohama, who, having been tricked into sleeping with Ryunosuke, then widowed by him, has to follow him when no one else will accept her. She is tied even closer to him when she bears his child. Faced with Ryunosuke's cruelty, Michiyo Aratama is particularly good at eliciting our sympathy for Ohama.

Based on the early chapters of a long, serialised novel, Shinobu

Hashimoto's script contains several clever devices. Skilful use of metaphor is woven into both the plot and the dialogue; Ryunosuke uses a cruel form of swordplay where he lures his victims in with a series of feints before delivering a single sudden and devastating blow. His teacher warns him of the dangers of using such a nasty form; a cruel sword leads to a cruel heart. This idea resonates throughout the plot, and forms the core message of Okamoto's film.

The final scenes of *Sword of Doom* are frighteningly violent, when Ryunosuke is ultimately driven mad by his cruel deeds, and goes on a violent rampage. The film's ending is appropriately abrupt and unpredictable.

THE VERDICT

Quite different to most samurai films, *Sword of Doom* is an entertaining examination of the consequences of cruelty for both the monster and his victims. With Kihachi Okamoto's talented direction, and a captivating performance by Tatsuya Nakadai, this is a prime example of the high quality of 1960s samurai cinema.

Samurai Rebellion (1967)

Japanese Title: *Joi-uchi: Hairyo tsuma shimatsu*
Written by: Adapted by Shinobu Hashimoto from the novel by Yasuhiko Takiguchi
Directed by: Masaki Kobayashi
Produced by: Tomoyuki Tanaka, Toshiro Mifune
Edited by: Hisashi Sagara
Cinematography: Kazuo Yamada
Cast: Toshiro Mifune (Isaburo), Tatsuya Nakadai (Tatewaki), Yoko Tsukasa (Ichi), Go Kato (Yogoro), Tatsuyoshi Ehara (Bunzo), Etsuko Ichihara (Kiku), Isao Yamagata (Shobei), Shigeru Koyama (Geki), Michiko Otsuka (Suga)

PLOT SUMMARY

When one of his concubines displeases him, Masakata, daimyo of the Aizu clan, orders that she marry Yogoro, the son of Isaburo, one of his samurai. Isaburo initially refuses, wanting Yogoro to avoid marrying for political convenience, as he did. However, Yogoro convinces his father that the marriage is for the best, and, surprisingly, he and his new wife, Ichi, fall in love and have a child, Tomi. This brings great delight to Isaburo, who till then had been miserable and constantly berated by his nasty wife, Suga. When Masakata's immediate heir dies unexpectedly, his child with Ichi, Kikuchiyo, becomes the new heir, and Masakata demands that Ichi be returned to him. Isaburo and Yogoro refuse, but Suga and Bunzo, Isaburo's other son, trick Ichi into returning to the castle, where she is held prisoner. Isaburo is ready to give up, but his friend Tatewaki, a border guard, convinces him not to. Masakata's chamberlain has Kiku, the wife of a low-ranking samurai, work for Isaburo as a wet nurse so that Tomi doesn't starve. Yogoro presents a petition for the return of Ichi, threatening to reveal Masakata's shameful behaviour to the rest of Japan. Masakata sends his steward, who arrives at Isaburo's house with Ichi, hoping to force them all to declare they are no longer related. Both men refuse, and Ichi responds by seizing a spear and killing herself. The steward's men attack, and kill Yogoro. Isaburo kills both the steward and his men, and heads for Edo with Tomi, hoping to tell the Shogunate of Masakata's shameful actions. Tatewaki blocks Isaburo's progress across the border, and the two agree to a duel, which Isaburo wins. In a final stand, Isaburo is killed by a large group of Masakata's men. Kiku rescues Tomi, adopting her as her own.

ANALYSIS

Samurai Rebellion is another moving film directed by Masaki Kobayashi, the talented filmmaker responsible for *Hara-kiri*. As in *Hara-kiri*,

Kobayashi chooses compelling subject matter which elicits an emotional response from his audience.

Like *Hara-kiri*, *Samurai Rebellion* tells a story of a man who refuses to adhere to the samurai code of unquestioning obedience, when he and his family are treated in an unjust and disgraceful way by his supposedly honourable superiors. Isaburo's grievances are utterly justified, having had a beloved daughter-in-law snatched away for purely political reasons. Though not as damning of the samurai code as *Hara-kiri*, this film does suggest that family is far more important than any code. Like Hanshiro in *Hara-kiri*, Isaburo is ready to sacrifice all for his family.

Isaburo makes for a very likeable, convincing character. Toshiro Mifune offers another great performance as a man who has given way on so many other matters, but refuses to jeopardise the happiness of the people who are most important in his life. Isaburo takes great delight in the happiness his son has found in married life (something he was never able to achieve), which Mifune conveys most movingly. He convincingly portrays Isaburo's transition from the unhappy man we meet at the beginning of the film into a much warmer character. His conviction adds weight to later scenes, when the family is in peril.

Samurai Rebellion also contains a memorable performance from the great Tatsuya Nakadai who is both likeable and disturbing as Tatewaki. Carefully limiting his expressions, vocally and facially, Nakadai is a man who carefully considers his actions. He only lets emotion creep into his performance in a few scenes, which consequently have great impact. In many ways Tatewaki is the opposite of Isaburo; where Mifune's character is emotional and expressive, Nakadai's isn't. It's a juxtaposition that works well, and results in some entertaining scenes between the two.

As in *Hara-kiri*, Kobayashi stages some frantic battle scenes. The duel between Isaburo and Tatewaki is a tense and unpredictable exchange of blows; by this point in their careers Mifune and Nakadai were both very experienced at swordplay. The scenes in which Isaburo battles the Aizu clan samurai are also very well constructed; Isaburo grows progressively more fatigued and wounded as he battles on; each time we think he has defeated his enemies, more appear from the thick undergrowth surrounding him, accompanied by the sound of gunshots.

THE VERDICT

Containing a compelling and moving story and perhaps the best ever pairing of stars Mifune and Nakadai, *Samurai Rebellion* is an indisputable classic of the samurai film genre.

Kill! (1968)

Japanese Title: *Kiru*
Directed by: Kihachi Okamoto
Written by: Adapted by Akira Murao and Kihachi Okamoto from the novel by Shugoro Yamamoto
Produced by: Tomoyuki Tanaka
Edited by: Yoshitami Kuroiwa
Cinematography: Rokuro Nishigaki
Cast: Tatsuya Nakadai (Genta), Etsushi Takahashi (Hanji), Naoko Kubo (Tetsutaro), Shigeru Koyama (Ayuzama), Akira Kubo (Monnosuke), Seishiro Kuno (Daijiro), Tadao Nakamaru (Shoda), Eijiro Tono (Hyogo), Isao Hashimoto (Konosuke), Yoshio Tsuchiya (Matsuo)

PLOT SUMMARY

A ronin, Hanji, and a yakuza, Genta, meet in an all but deserted town. There they become embroiled in the efforts of a group of seven samurai to wipe out the corruption from their clan. As it turns out, Hanji is in fact a peasant who hopes to become a samurai, and Genta is a ronin, having rejected samurai life by choice, and now travelling in disguise. The seven samurai become trapped in a small building, surrounded by their enemies. Hanji falls in with a group of ronin working for the conspirators, promised samurai status if they succeed in dislodging the seven honest samurai. The clan figure behind the corruption actually plans to kill them all, hoping to remove all evidence of his deeds. Genta reveals this plot to Hanji, who is forced to reconsider his aspirations to join the world of the samurai. Through Genta's machinations the conspirators are defeated, and Hanji decides that the samurai life is not for him after all.

ANALYSIS

Kill! is an interesting example of the samurai film, one that ventures much further into comedy than other films in the genre. However, combined with the comedy is an effective criticism of the unquestioning obedience of the samurai code. The plot of *Kill!* is derived from the same novel that inspired Kurosawa's *Sanjuro*, but the two films are structured quite differently. Although both concern a ronin assisting a group of samurai against their corrupt superiors, the actual mechanics of the two plots are quite different. *Kill!* revolves around two swordsmen, Genta and Hanji, and their differing experiences of the samurai lifestyle, rather than focusing on one protagonist, as Kurosawa does in *Sanjuro*.

The tone of *Kill!* is very different to director Kihachi Okamoto's sombre masterpiece, *Sword of Doom*. Here Okamoto proves his versatility, and despite its darkness, the humour in *Kill!* is always amusing. The scenes involving the simple and unruly Hanji (Etsushi Takahashi) and his visit to a brothel are hilarious, due to Takahashi's exuberant performance and Okamoto's clever use of simple gags. The flamboyant soundtrack also adds much to the overall comedic tone, punctuating humorous scenes with quick beats of music, reminiscent of the great Ennio Morricone.

Similarly, Tatsuya Nakadai is highly entertaining as Genta, the vagabond who is never without a wry response. It's evidence of his considerable range as an actor: the immensely likeable character he plays here is polar opposite to the cruelty he plays in films such as *Yojimbo*, *Sanjuro* and *Sword of Doom*.

Hanji (Etsushi Takahashi) and Genta (Tatsuya Nakadai); both very hungry. *Kill!* directed by Kihachi Okamoto and produced by Tomoyuki Tanaka for Toho Studios.

Okamoto's film is far more than a series of gags. There is a clever interplay throughout, regarding truth and appearance. Right from the beginning of the film, people are not as they seem. Playing with typical samurai film archetypes, many characters are actually disguised, so the character we think we recognise is someone different. This notion of deception is also woven more directly into the film's plot with the main villain constantly using subterfuge and untruths to his advantage.

Okamoto also criticises the unquestioning obedience of the samurai, but in a far gentler manner than Masaki Kobayashi does in *Hara-kiri*. Genta's life has been badly affected by the samurai code, and as he and Hanji become involved in events reminiscent of his past, Genta slowly educates Hanji on the shortcomings of being a samurai. The revelation of Genta's past acts as a final denouncement of unquestioning obedience, and, in this respect, *Kill!* is much less sentimental than many samurai films.

The dire results of this compliance, mainly needless violence, are handled well within *Kill!* As you might expect from such a title, there is plenty of action. The sword fighting is fast and frantic, with plenty of grizzly special effects.

THE VERDICT

Kill! is similar to *Sanjuro* in its combination of brutal violence and amusing set pieces. However, *Kill!* exaggerates both these features to new levels, which clearly distinguishes it from Kurosawa's film. *Kill!* is thoroughly entertaining, for both those familiar with samurai films and those new to the genre.

Red Lion (1969)

Japanese Title: *Akage*
Directed by: Kihachi Okamoto
Written by: Sakae Hirosawa, Kihachi Okamoto
Produced by: Toshiro Mifune, Yoshio Nishikawa
Edited by: Yoshihiro Araki
Cinematography: Takao Saito
Cast: Toshiro Mifune (Gonzo), Shiwa Iwashita (Tomi), Etsushi Takahashi (Hanzo), Minori Terada (Sanji), Nobuko Otowa (Oharu), Yuko Mochizuki (Ume), Jitsuko Yoshimura (Oyoo), Kawai Okada (Osode), Shigeru Koyama (Aragaki), Hideo Amamoto (Dr. Gensai), Tokue Hanazawa (Komotora)

PLOT SUMMARY

Gonzo, a peasant, has recently joined the Imperial Force, an army raised by the Emperor to oppose the Shogunate. Promising lower taxes and cancellation of debts, the Imperial Force is having no trouble winning over village after village as they move though Japan. Gonzo, a rather simple but very tough warrior, is bored by all these peaceful conquests, and asks to go on ahead to his home village, which he believes he can easily win over to the Imperial cause. His commander allows this, and even lends Gonzo his red lion headdress, a mane of bright red, to give him authority in his efforts. Arriving in Sawado, Gonzo uses his new authority to release the villagers from a variety of different debts, and free his wife from prostitution, but makes enemies of the local magistrate and yakuza in doing so. There is also a mysterious group of samurai, hoping to protect the interests of the Shogunate. The Imperial Force turns out to be a farce; the promises of lower taxes are false, used to secure the support of the peasants. Gonzo and his wife are both killed by the Imperial troops, which spurs the peasants into action, as they refuse the Imperial Force entry into Sawado.

ANALYSIS

Based loosely on real events in Japanese history, Kihachi Okamoto's *Red Lion* is a moving film about the lower classes (in this case, peasants) and their manipulation by those in power. This is among the most anti-authoritarian of Okamoto's films, which usually focus on flaws within an individual, rather than an institution. While it may sound like heavy viewing, *Red Lion* is a well-balanced combination of comedy and heart-wrenching tragedy.

Toshiro Mifune's performance as Gonzo is the key to the success of *Red Lion*. This is Mifune at his blustering best; in Gonzo, Mifune creates a character who is charming in his energetic enthusiasm and naivety, and the audience cannot help but like him. Arriving in his village of Sawado, Gonzo sets about making trouble for the local authorities, mainly the local samurai policeman (a coward at heart), his deputies and the local extortionists and moneylenders. In a series of highly comedic scenes, Gonzo frees women who have been sold into prostitution by their indebted families and destroys ten years' worth of recorded peasant debts. However, Gonzo is far more than just a comedic character. Mifune adds extra depth to his performance, in particular when Gonzo is touchingly reunited with his wife and mother after a ten-year absence. Gonzo's motivations are clearly quite pure; he truly believes in the 'world renewal' propaganda spouted by the Imperial Force and wants to make a better life for the peasants and his family.

The emotional investment Mifune forces us to put into his character makes the last quarter of the film all the more tragic. Events take a turn for the worse in Sawado. Hanzo, a ronin staying in Sawado, is proved correct in his cynical attitude to the Imperial Force. As such, the entire film could be seen as cynical, an opinion that's reinforced by its enthusiastic, comedic beginning and violent, tragic end. The Imperial Force isn't at all what it promised to be, and some of the film's most endearing characters die as a result of this betrayal. However, the final moments of the film, sad as they are, are ultimately uplifting because they show what Gonzo was able to inspire in his hometown.

THE VERDICT

Red Lion is an entertaining blend of tragedy and humour, well worth seeing for Mifune's amusing performance and Okamoto's moving direction.

Samurai Banners (1969)

Japanese Title: *Furin kazan*
Directed by: Hiroshi Inagaki
Written by: Adapted by Shinobu Hashimoto and Takeo Kunihiro from the novel by Yasushi Inoue
Produced by: Hiroshi Inagaki, Toshiro Mifune, Yoshio Nishikawa, Tomoyuki Tanaka
Edited by: Yoshihiro Araki
Cinematography: Kazuo Yamada
Cast: Toshiro Mifune (Kansuke Yamamoto), Yoshiko Sakuma (Princess Yu), Kinnosuke Nakamura (Shingen Takeda), Yujiro Ishihara (Kenshin Uesugi), Katsuo Nakamura (Nobusato Itagaki), Kanemon Nakamura (Nobukato Itagaki), Kankuro Nakamura (Katsuyori Takeda)

PLOT SUMMARY

A ronin named Kansuke Yamamoto uses considerable guile and cunning to secure a position with Shingen Takeda, a powerful daimyo. Kansuke helps Shingen defeat one of his rivals, Suwa, by making overtures of peace, then having the man killed when he visits Shingen's castle. When Shingen marches on Suwa's lands, Kansuke finds Yu, Suwa's daughter, who he takes into his own home. Shingen takes Yu as his concubine, much to his wife Sanjo's distaste. Yu resents being a concubine, but Kansuke convinces her she must, so that she can bear a son to Shingen, and the Suwa and Takeda blood can be combined. Yu does have a son by Takeda, named Shiro. Kansuke grows very close to them both, and manipulates matters so that Shiro becomes Takeda's heir. With his ingenious use of tactics, Kansuke helps Shingen defeat many of his rivals. As more battles take place, a showdown with Kenshin Uesugi, Shingen's most powerful rival, becomes more and more inevitable. Kansuke prepares a castle where he believes the battle will take place, hoping that Shiro will be old enough to command when it does. Kenshin arrives with a large army, and Kansuke wants to stay in the castle, luring Kenshin into a trap. However, Shingen insists on a direct attack, which Kansuke plans. For the first time, his tactics are ineffective, and Kenshin very nearly kills Shingen. Kansuke dies in the battle, and Shingen mocks him, saying he was blinded by his love for Yu and Shiro.

ANALYSIS

The last of Hiroshi Inagaki's historical films, *Samurai Banners* was filmed on a suitably grand scale. A great example of an epic historical film, it tells the story of Takeda Shingen, a daimyo who actually lived and is famous for his many conquests during feudal Japan's long succession of civil wars. Interestingly, this film fits together quite well with Kurosawa's *Kagemusha*, which details Takeda's death and the fate of the Shingen clan. *Samurai Banners* is concerned with some of Takeda's most famous battles, and the ruthless samurai who helped him win them, Kansuke Yamamoto.

What stands out most about this film are the lavish battle scenes, achieved through the use of large numbers of extras, all immaculately costumed and armed. Inagaki is no stranger to directing large-scale battle scenes, and doesn't fail to deliver in this film. The battles are well edited, and seem realistic, an admirable quality in an historical film. Inagaki creates a sense of the confusion of warfare, filling the frame with extras, all flailing wildly at each other, desperately trying to stay alive. We see some magnificent sights – rousing cavalry charges, and huge infantry clashes – and, as usual, Inagaki should be commended for his grasp of epic subject matter. Some of the battle scenes are more reminiscent of the over-the-top style of combat seen in the *Lone Wolf and Cub* series: the scene in which three soldiers carry a huge blade, and run in a circle, creating something like an enormous blender, is highly entertaining. Fortunately, such scenes do not detract from the epic feel of the entire film.

The lives of Shingen and Kansuke make for interesting viewing, whether you're familiar with the history or not. Both men demonstrate the level of ruthlessness which must have been necessary for a samurai to succeed in such uncertain times. While this is refreshingly realistic, it also makes it difficult for the audience to actually like them. Kansuke, who is clearly supposed to be a sympathetic character, in particular suffers from this. Despite a skilled performance by Toshiro Mifune, it is difficult to feel sorry for Kansuke at the film's conclusion, when he has shown so little regard for human life. As such, *Samurai Banners* is not as moving as other Inagaki's *Samurai Trilogy* and *The 47 Ronin*.

THE VERDICT

Not as touching as Inagaki's other work, *Samurai Banners* contains some epic battle scenes and a compelling story lifted from the pages of

Japan's turbulent history. If you're in the mood for a larger-than-life tale, then this is the film for you.

THE 1970s

The popularity of samurai films lasted into the 1970s, although the genre started to lose ground to the increasingly popular yakuza (gangster) films.

During the 1970s, the genre was heavily influenced by Japanese comics (manga), many of which were adapted into live-action films. These films shared the over-the-top action and characters of their source material, and took the graphic violence of the 1960s films even further. The manga-inspired films were wonderfully overblown, and didn't take themselves too seriously, resulting in simple entertainment that was beautiful to look at. The most famous of these films are the *Lone Wolf and Cub* series, featuring Itto Ogami, his baby son Daigoro and a baby cart concealing an arsenal of deadly weapons. Others include the *Lady Snowblood* and *Hanzo the Razor* series. There is more to these films than just the action; the *Lady Snowblood* films in particular have a definite point to make.

The *Zatoichi* series continued into the 1970s, also influenced in part by the style of manga-inspired films. This is not surprising, considering that Shintaro Katsu's (the star of the *Zatoichi* films) production company was responsible for both *Lone Wolf and Cub* and the *Zatoichi* films of the 1970s.

Incident at Blood Pass (1970)

Japanese Title: *Machibuse*
Directed by: Hiroshi Inagaki
Written by: Yumi Fujiki, Hideo Oguni, Hajime Takaiwa, Ichiro Miyagawa
Produced by: Toshiro Mifune, Yoshio Nishikawa
Edited by: Yoshihiro Araki
Cinematography: Kazuo Yamada
Cast: Toshiro Mifune (the Ronin), Yujiro Ishihara (Yataro), Ruriko Asaoka (Okuni), Shintaro Katsu (Gentetsu), Kinnosuke Nakamura (Heima), Chusha Ichikawa (samurai leader), Ichiro Arishima (Tokubei), Mika Kitagawa (Oyuki), Yoshio Tsuchiya (Itahachi), Jotaro Togami (Gonji)

PLOT SUMMARY

A nameless ronin receives a strange assignment from his new employer. He is to proceed to a desolate mountain pass and wait for something to happen. His employer, a mysterious samurai, tells him he will know when the time is right to act. Arriving at the pass the ronin stays at a small inn and meets a series of interesting characters. Among them are a young gambler, a criminal, an inspector, a young woman the ronin saves from her abusive husband, and a mysterious physician, hiding away from the world. Through a series of events it becomes clear what is really happening at the pass: Gentetsu, the physician, is in fact a samurai also hired by the ronin's employer, his mission being to ambush a caravan carrying Shogunate gold. Gentetsu takes control of the inn with a gang of thugs and the ronin's real mission is delivered to him; his employer wants Gentetsu dead and the ronin is to kill him. The caravan is completely fake, all to lure Gentetsu into a trap. Enraged by the betrayal of his mysterious employer, the ronin attempts to save Gentetsu, who throws himself down a gorge, preferring to die than be captured. The ronin leaves the pass alone and kills his employer, in vengeance for all the bloodshed he has caused.

ANALYSIS

Incident at Blood Pass is a character-driven film, set amid majestic snow-capped mountains. The way these characters interact makes up much of the first half of the film, and their exchanges are both well written and acted. The film's writing team have created an interesting blend of characters, whose differing perspectives often act as an examination of justice, one of the central themes of *Incident at Blood Pass*. Mifune's ronin is a compassionate man, taking great pains to avoid killing his adversaries in combat. He has his own sense of justice, choosing to viciously strike down those he believes deserve death. Yujiro Ishihara plays Yataro, a tough young gambler, who despises the law and thieves alike. Shintaro Katsu, famous for his long-running role as Zatochi the blind swordsman, here plays Gentetsu, a seemingly uncouth ex-physician, hiding away from the world for his own reasons. The two women at the inn, Okuni and Oyuki, are both merciful and tolerant, and prefer not to see harm come to anyone. This is particularly poignant for Okuni who, badly beaten by her husband, still begs the ronin not to kill him, and shows concern when he is injured later in the film.

When an inspector and the criminal he was chasing arrive at the inn, both nearly dead from their wounds, the theme of justice is examined more thoroughly. Gentetsu shows great apathy in refusing to treat them but is spurred into action by the ronin and Oyuki. When he regains consciousness the inspector treats his prisoner with great brutality, beating him and making him eat like a dog, all the while refusing him water. He claims to do this in the name of justice. It's hard not to take a strange sense of enjoyment from a later scene, where the thief is freed and savagely beats the inspector, which seems far more just than the earlier tortures.

The second half of the film contains some unpredictable twists, which ultimately lead to violence. The fight scenes are well choreographed, both frenetic and chaotic, which adds a sense of realism, even though there is very little blood and gore on display.

Although the content of this film is different to the historical epics he usually directed, Hiroshi Inagaki created an entertaining film from this compelling material. In particular, he makes good use of the scenic backdrop of the snowy mountain pass, in many ways reminiscent of the grand landscapes of his other films.

THE VERDICT

All in all, *Incident at Blood Pass* is a great samurai film, containing clever characterisation, thought-provoking themes and skilled direction.

Zatoichi Meets Yojimbo (1970)

Japanese Title: *Zatoichi to Yojimbo*
Directed by: Kihachi Okamoto
Written by: Adapted by Kihachi Okamoto and Tetsuro Yoshida from a story by Kan Shimozawa
Produced by: Shintaro Katsu, Hiroyoshi Nishioka
Edited by: Toshio Taniguchi
Cinematography: Kazuo Miyagawa
Cast: Shintaro Katsu (Zatoichi), Toshiro Mifune (Sasa the yojimbo), Ayako Wakao (Umeno), Osamu Takizawa (Eboshiya), Masakane Sakatoshi (Masagoro), Shin Kishida (Kuzuryu), Kanjuro Arashi (Hyoroku), Toshiyuki Hosokawa (Sanyemon)

PLOT SUMMARY

Needing a break from his violent lifestyle, Zatoichi returns to a village he has fond memories of. He finds the village a much more sombre place now, with a yakuza boss, Masagoro, and his father, Eboshiya, fighting over a hidden stash of gold stolen from the Shogunate. Masagoro has hired Sasa, a samurai, as his yojimbo (bodyguard). After Zatoichi roughs up some of his men, Masagoro sends Sasa after him, but the two end up having a drink instead. Sasa is in love with Umeno, the young woman who runs the sake house. Attacks by Sasa and Masagoro's men on Eboshiya's house and warehouse both fail to reveal the location of the gold. Kuzuryu, a skilled warrior, arrives to protect Eboshiya, sent by Sanyemon, his other son, who originally sent the stolen gold from Edo. It becomes clear that both Sasa and Kuzuryu are agents of the Shogun, attempting to recover the gold. Meanwhile, Zatoichi discovers that the gold is hidden inside the 130 small Buddha statues that Eboshiya had made for the village shrine. A large battle between Eboshiya and Masagoro's gangs erupts, and Zatoichi takes advantage of the confusion to gather all the gold dust in a large pile outside the village gates. Sasa attempts to arrest Eboshiya, but Sanyemon, trying to kill him, wounds his father. The battle subsides as Eboshiya, Masagoro and Sanyemon all make for the gold. Kuzuryu kills them all with a pistol, wanting the gold for himself. Sasa kills him, but not before Umeno is shot. Sasa attempts to save Umeno, but believing it's hopeless, he and Zatoichi begin to fight. Umeno regains consciousness, and the two stop fighting. Both Zatoichi and Sasa attempt to get the gold, which all blows away in the wind. Zatoichi leaves Sasa to take care of Umeno.

ANALYSIS

Zatoichi Meets Yojimbo combines two of the most enduring characters in samurai films: Shintaro Katsu's affable Zatoichi and Toshiro Mifune's gruff but likeable yojimbo. The two meet in a village which hides a fortune in stolen gold. Not only do they have greedy yakuza to contend with, but also each other.

A co-production between Toho and Shintaro Katsu's production company, the greatest feature of *Zatoichi Meets Yojimbo* is its two leading men. As in *Incident at Blood Pass*, they make a wonderful combination, and are even more entertaining here. Mifune and Katsu play up the rivalry between their characters very well; their interplay is always entertaining, whether they're insulting, threatening or trying to fool each other. The often sly humour of Katsu's Zatoichi and the blustering, sometimes drunken, outbursts of Mifune's yojimbo are a delicious mix, which writer and director Kihachi Okamoto never misses an opportunity to exploit.

Indeed, this film contains much more comedy than most Zatoichi films; the scenes with Sasa (the yojimbo) and the bumbling yakuza he associates with are always amusing, particularly the way Sasa continually imitates them. Similarly, Zatoichi himself is funnier, accidentally knocking himself out when trying to escape the local lawman and trying to fake death spasms with amusing results.

At no point does this tone detract from the more serious scenes, yet *Zatoichi Meets Yojimbo* is not without its faults. The plot has so many twists and turns that it could potentially confuse and irritate viewers, rather than surprise them. This is unusual coming from Kihachi Okamoto, the talented director responsible for classic samurai films such as *Samurai Assassin*, *Sword of Doom* and *Kill!* It looks as though Okamoto tried to put a little too much into the plot; with a shorter running time and fewer twists, *Zatoichi Meets Yojimbo* could have been every bit as entertaining as his other work.

The battle scenes are also slightly disappointing. While Katsu and Mifune draw on their unique styles, they have both done much better work in other films. Similarly, the large-scale battle between the two yakuza factions towards the end is not up to Okamoto's usual standards. The battles between Zatoichi and Sasa are not without merit, but seem somewhat anti-climactic.

THE VERDICT

Despite disappointing on some levels, *Zatoichi Meets Yojimbo* is interesting viewing for samurai film fans simply because it combines two of the genre's most popular characters, and is worth seeing alone for Katsu and Mifune's entertaining interaction.

Zatoichi: The Festival of Fire (1970)

Japanese Title: *Zatoichi abare-himatsuri*
Directed by: Kenji Misumi
Written by: Adapted by Takayuki Yamada and Shintaro Katsu from a story by Kan Shimozawa
Produced by: Shintaro Katsu
Edited by: Toshio Taniguchi
Cinematography: Kazuo Miyagawa
Cast: Shintaro Katsu (Zatoichi), Tatsuya Nakadai (ronin), Reiko Ohara (Okiyo), Masayuki Mori (Yamikubo), Peter (Umeji)

PLOT SUMMARY

Zatoichi, the famed blind swordsman, rescues a beautiful woman from a mistress auction. She doesn't get far; a mysterious ronin finds and kills her. Attending the promotion ceremony for a local yakuza boss, Kuroko, Zatoichi is disrespectful, but the angry men are stopped by their supreme leader, Yamikubo, another blind man referred to as the shogun of the underworld. Yamikubo holds a vote among the yakuza bosses, and it is decided that Zatoichi must be killed. Several attempts fail, and the yakuza send Okiyo, a pretty young girl, to lure Zatoichi into their trap. Zatoichi meets the ronin, who accuses him of sleeping with his wife. The ronin has killed everyone else she slept with, and mistakenly believes Zatoichi did after he rescued her. The ronin promises they will duel soon. Okiyo and Zatoichi form a bond, and she tries to convince him not to attend the festival to which Yamikubo has invited him. Umeji, a young pimp Zatoichi befriends, unsuccessfully attempts to seduce and kill him. Arriving at the festival, Zatoichi is lured into a cunning trap. He escapes and succeeds in killing Yamikubo, but not before Okiyo's family are murdered by the yakuza boss. The ronin arrives and saves Zatoichi from Yamikubo's many henchmen. Zatoichi and the ronin duel, and Zatoichi emerges victorious. Seeing the way love ruined the ronin's life, Zatoichi chooses not to have Okiyo accompany him, even though she wants to.

ANALYSIS

Zatoichi: The Festival of Fire is an entertaining film and high point in the series. With the usual amiable performance from Katsu, the assured direction of Kenji Misumi and a great performance from the immensely talented genre veteran Tatsuya Nakadai, it's one of Zatoichi's best adventures.

Kenji Misumi, the director responsible for the early Zatoichi films, who would go on to direct the best of the *Lone Wolf and Cub* series, handles the material with the skill and assurance that samurai film fans have come to expect. Misumi creates some wonderful scenes in this film. The amusing opening sequence in which Zatoichi tries to get rid of a pesky dog, the scene where Zatoichi pulls Okiyo along in a cart and the blind swordsman's rude arrival at a yakuza gathering are all classic Zatoichi, that entirely utilise Katsu's charismatic performance.

Misumi also makes sure he doesn't waste the talents of Tatsuya Nakadai, who puts in a tour-de-force performance as a ronin driven mad by his cheating wife; the kind of character he is famous for – an unnerving and inexpressive individual completely fixated on his violent goals. Similar to the characters he played in films such as *Sanjuro* and *Sword of Doom*, Nakadai's cold stare, conveyed through his large eyes, is no less chilling here. Particularly memorable is the sequence in which the ronin, having drunk a lot of sake, finds himself reliving the events which changed his life forever. Shot against a stark white background, these scenes consist of very quick cuts of the ronin discovering his wife with another man, who he kills, before commencing the vengeful pursuit of his wife, for which he sacrifices his position as a Shogunate samurai. The sight of Nakadai, a look of horror and anger stretched across his face, made mesmerising by the blank background, is an image the viewer will not soon forget. Such highly stylised images show a talent that would become evident in Misumi's later work on the *Lone Wolf and Cub* films.

Another strength is the film's intriguing villain, Yamikubo, the blind lord of the yakuza. Zatoichi and Yamikubo share a variety of interesting and amusing lines on the subject of their blindness, but Yamikubo turns out to be every bit as ruthless (perhaps more so) as any other yakuza boss. Masayuki Mori plays this character very well, fashioning a credible rival for Zatoichi, and deserving of his rage.

Like all Zatoichi films, *The Festival of Fire* contains the requisite battle scenes. The incident when Zatoichi is attacked by a large group of naked yakuza in a bathhouse is as brutal as it is bizarre, and the climactic scene, in which he's trapped by his enemies on a platform in the middle of a pool, makes for a tense spectacle, particularly when oil in the pool is set alight, trapping Zatoichi in a ring of fire.

THE VERDICT

This is a great film to watch if you've never seen any Zatoichi films; everything that made the series such a success is present. Highly recommended.

Lone Wolf and Cub: Sword of Vengeance (1972)

Japanese Title: *Kozure Okami: Kowokashi udekashi tsukamatsuru*
Directed by: Kenji Misumi
Written by: Adapted by Kazuo Koike from the manga he created with Goseki Kojima
Produced by: Shintaro Katsu, Hisaharu Matsubara
Edited by: Toshio Taniguchi
Cinematography: Chishi Makiura

Cast: Tomisaburo Wakayama (Itto Ogami), Fumio Watanabe (Sugito), Tomoko Mayama (Osen), Shigeru Tsuyuguchi (Matsuki), Reiko Kasahara (Azami), Akihiro Tomikawa (Daigoro), Tokio Oki (Retsudo Yagyu)

PLOT SUMMARY

Itto Ogami was once the Shogun's second, his job to assist daimyos who have offended the Shogun in committing seppuku. The Yagyu clan, jealous of his position, murder his wife and attempt to frame him for disrespectful behaviour towards the Shogunate. Itto and his infant son survive, and both embark on the path of the assassin, hoping to eventually inflict their revenge on the Yagyu. Itto meets with Ichige Gyobu, a chamberlain of the Oyamada clan, who wants to hire him as an assassin. He wants Itto to kill Sugito, a chamberlain who is attempting to gain control of the Oyamada clan by assassinating the current lord. Itto reaches the village where Sugito waits to ambush the Oyamada daimyo. Itto is confronted by some of Sugito's ronin. He does not resist them as they take his sword, beat him and force him to pleasure Osen, a prostitute. Ready to leave to perform their duties for Sugito, the ronin plan to kill all the travellers in the village, but Itto intervenes, using weapons cleverly concealed in the baby cart in which he pushes Daigoro around. Kanbei, the leader of the ronin, realises who Itto is, but it's too late. Itto kills Kanbei, Sugito and all their men, before quietly leaving the village. Osen attempts to follow him, but Itto threatens to cut the bridge she stands on, and she lets him go on his way.

ANALYSIS

There is something undeniably cool about an assassin pushing his child around in a deadly baby cart. Welcome to the wonderfully overblown world of *Lone Wolf and Cub*, where the action is fast, graphic and violent.

The first film in the popular *Lone Wolf and Cub* series, *Sword of*

Vengeance, is a good beginning, but doesn't reach the giddy heights of *Baby Cart on the River Styx*, the second and best film in the series. *Sword of Vengeance* is primarily concerned with how Itto and Daigoro came to be the wandering assassins known as Lone Wolf and Cub, and as such is more concerned with the backstory than the simple and violent tales the series excels in.

A co-production between Toho and Shintaro 'Zatoichi' Katsu's production company, *Sword of Vengeance* stars Katsu's brother, Tomisaburo Wakayama, as Ogami Itto, a role in which he excels. Like the Zatoichi films, the *Lone Wolf and Cub* series derives much of its appeal from its solid central character and one actor's unforgettable portrayal of him. Wakayama's Itto is a stern, inexpressive man, whose features rarely change. He's unemotional, having chosen a path of death and vengeance which he sticks to with the same inexpressive stoicism he uses to follow the code of bushido. It is Wakayama's inexpressiveness that makes him so memorable; his cold, emotionless stare through narrowed eyes drills through the toughest of opponents, and never fails to impress, no matter how many times you watch the film. There is one scene which is a classic example of Wakayama's Itto: the scene in which Itto places his sword and a colourful ball on the floor and tells Daigoro, his infant son, to choose his destiny by crawling towards one; the sword means he embarks on the assassin's life with his father, the ball means he joins his dead mother. Wakayama plays this scene with such conviction that you really believe Itto has no qualms about killing his child, as he wishes to spare his son the harsh life of vengeance he is about to undertake. When Itto occasionally does show emotion, such as the slight hint of amusement he gives when he defeats Gyubo's men, it's a mere glimmer through Wakayama's stone-like features. Young Akihiro Tomikawa also offers an assured performance as Daigoro, Itto's little son, but is used to much greater effect in the next film, *Baby Cart on the River Styx*.

Interestingly, *Sword of Vengeance* is directed by Kenji Misumi, who helmed the first Zatoichi film, there at the beginning of two of samurai films' most enduring characters. Misumi is true to the popular manga which inspired the *Lone Wolf and Cub* films, carefully creating a series of beautifully composed shots. The image of water coursing over Itto's sword as it is cleaned in preparation for an execution and the bloodied fingers of Azami touching Daigoro's cheek as she dies are just two examples of the violent yet graceful shots that Misumi offers his audience.

Of course, the cornerstone of the *Lone Wolf and Cub* series is flamboyant manga-styled battle scenes, and *Sword of Vengeance* well and truly delivers. Wakayama proves to be just as competent as his brother at hacking his way through hordes of enemies, and the scenes in which he does are highly entertaining. The gory effects, such as frequent blood sprays and severed limbs, make them gloriously grotesque. Particularly good is the final battle in which Itto takes on Kanbei and his ronin. Misumi builds a great sense of anticipation, and when the battle occurs it's full of gory surprises.

THE VERDICT

Not as good as its sequel, *Sword of Vengeance* is nevertheless a worthy film. If you intend to watch the entire *Lone Wolf and Cub* series then this is the place to start.

Lone Wolf and Cub: Baby Cart on the River Styx (1972)

Japanese Title: *Kozure Okami: Sanzu no kawa no ubaguruma*
Directed by: Kenji Misumi
Written by: Adapted by Kazuo Koike from the manga he created with Goseki Kojima
Produced by: Shintaro Katsu, Hisaharu Matsubara
Edited by: Toshio Taniguchi
Cinematography: Chishi Makiura
Cast: Tomisaburo Wakayama (Itto Ogami), Kayo Matsuo (Sayaka), Akiji

Kobayashi (Benma Hidari), Minoru Ohki (Tenma Hidari), Shin Kishida (Kuruma Hidari), Akihiro Tomikawa (Daigoro)

PLOT SUMMARY

Ogami Itto's deadly enemies from the previous film, the Yagyu clan, are still after him. This time utilising two skilled teams of shinobi (ninja) from their ranks, one all male, the other all female, the Yagyu hope to eliminate Itto once and for all. Itto has continued on the path of the assassin that he chose in the first film, and still takes his little son Daigoro with him everywhere. This time, Itto accepts a contract to kill a dye-maker who threatens to ruin a lucrative monopoly held by a small clan. His target is protected by the three Hidari brothers, the highly skilled, official escorts of the Shogunate. Itto nearly fails in his mission, and is almost killed by the shinobi. Daigoro nurses him back to health but is then captured by the surviving shinobi, and is almost drowned before Itto rescues him. Following the Hidari brothers onto a boat, Itto and Daigoro must escape from a fire lit by thugs trying to kill the Hidari, and survive the cold night by sharing body warmth with Sayaka, the only survivor of the female shinobi. Sayaka finds it increasingly hard to harm Itto, mainly because of Daigoro. Catching up with the Hidari brothers, Itto kills them in a bloody battle and completes his mission by killing the dye-maker. Sayaka confronts him one last time, but cannot bring herself to fight him.

ANALYSIS

Baby Cart on the River Styx is considered by many to be the best of the *Lone Wolf and Cub* series, and for good reason. With the backstory told in *Sword of Vengeance* (1972), this film is free to tell its bloody tale. Itto and Daigoro must contend with two teams of deadly shinobi (ninja), one male, one female, and the highly skilled Hidari brothers, otherwise known as the Masters of Death.

The simple plot is one of the film's best assets. Presenting a series of causes and effects, the plot never feels as if it's crudely assembled around the violence, which is sometimes the case with *zankoku eiga* (cruel films). The characters all have sufficient motivation to carry out their violent acts. The Yagyu clan, for example, feel it is vital to eliminate Ogami because he's humiliated them; this is expressed simply through their anger as they discuss events. The Hidari brothers, for their part, are charged to protect by the Shogun, a duty they take very seriously.

Like the other *Lone Wolf and Cub* films, the most obvious feature of *Baby Cart on the River Styx* is its graphic violence. This film is not for the squeamish. Buckets of blood, along with a multitude of body parts, are flung all over the screen. But with its manga origins, it is only natural that the *Lone Wolf and Cub* series should inherit this gory, heightened violence. Director Kenji Misumi uses quick cuts, never lingering too long on any individual violent act, creating rapid montages of bloody combat which have an incredibly appealing visceral nature. During the battle scenes a variety of exotic weapons are on display, not least the baby cart itself, which conceals Ogami's considerable arsenal. The choreography creates smooth-flowing exchanges; the scene in which Itto dispatches most of the male shinobi is one such example; he reacts quickly to the attacks of his multiple opponents, moving rapidly from one to the next, fighting them on different levels (from above, below, and so on).

As much attention is paid to characterisation as action. Though low on dialogue, the film's central characters are cleverly designed, and prove to be intriguing in their own right. This is assisted greatly by performances from a talented cast. Ogami Itto (Tomisaburo Wakayama) continues to be an interesting protagonist. His face seems permanently frozen, a sign of the horrors he has faced. Largely unexpressive, he's able to convey a great deal with a simple glance or slight movement of his brows. This is a far cry from the highly expressive heroes that usually feature in samurai films, portrayed by actors such as Toshiro Mifune, Shintaro Katsu and Tatsuya Nakadai.

The villains in this film, Sayaka and her female shinobi in particular, are wonderfully exaggerated, presenting comic-book evil at its best, a pleasing contrast with Itto's constant stern expression.

Special mention must be made of Akihiro Tomikawa, the child actor who plays Daigoro, Itto's little son. Only five or six years old, he gives an amazing performance, and matches his father's cold stare. Yet he also retains childlike qualities, which makes for an interesting juxtaposition; in one scene he helps his father deal with some shinobi, then in the next he points and laughs at a scarecrow. The scenes in which Daigoro helps nurse his father back to health are touching, and contrast well with the visceral violence that has just taken place.

THE VERDICT

If you only see one film from the *Lone Wolf and Cub* series, make sure it's *Baby Cart on the River Styx*. This film combines all the best elements of the series, including gory fight scenes, entertaining scripting and skilled performances from Wakayama and Tomikawa.

Lone Wolf and Cub: Baby Cart to Hades (1972)

Japanese Title: *Kozure Okami: Shinikazeni mukau ubaguruma*
Directed by: Kenji Misumi
Written by: Adapted by Kazuo Koike from the manga he created with Goseki Kojima
Produced by: Shintaro Katsu, Hisaharu Matsubara
Edited by: Toshio Taniguchi
Cinematography: Chishi Makiura
Cast: Tomisaburo Wakayama (Itto Ogami), Go Kato (Kanbei), Yuko Hamada (Torizo), Isao Yamagata (Genba), Akihiro Tomikawa (Daigoro)

PLOT SUMMARY

Itto Ogami and his son Daigoro continue to travel the path of the assassin. They encounter Ometsu, a young girl who has been sold to the yakuza as a sex slave and is trying to escape. Itto refuses to hand her over to Torizo, a tough female yakuza boss, when he sees the girl carries a memorial tablet, which reminds him of the tablet which ruined his own life. Eventually Itto agrees to undergo the torturous process that Ometsu must complete to be free of the yakuza, in her place. Surviving the tortures, although badly beaten, Itto then accepts an assignment from Torizo's father, Miura, who is in fact a ronin. Miura wants Itto to kill Genba, the man who betrayed his clan, causing it to be dissolved. Itto agrees and sets off to complete this mission. Genba also attempts to hire Itto to kill his superior, who he fears is plotting against him, but Itto refuses. He kills Genba's two most skilled samurai. Genba raises a small army to hunt the assassin. Itto confronts the army, and through a combination of heavy firepower, concealed in the baby cart, and his great skill, defeats them, killing Genba himself. A ronin named Kanbei then steps forward to challenge Itto, having been hired by Genba. Itto defeats him, and Kanbei recounts his tale, where he was shunned by his clan for leaving his lord's side to protect him. Itto applauds his actions and acts as his second as he commits seppuku. Torizo, who has watched the entire battle, tries to follow Itto, but is restrained by her men, who fear for her safety.

ANALYSIS

Not as enjoyable as *Baby Cart on the River Styx*, *Baby Cart to Hades* is nevertheless a strong entry in the series. Featuring more exaggerated comic-book violence, this is the first film in which Itto takes on an entire army.

This film puts Itto into a number of new situations, the most interesting of which takes place when he and Daigoro help Ometsu, a girl who is to be sold to a brothel. The plight of the innocent is not usually something Itto concerns himself with, not part of the assassin's path he has chosen. This predicament leads to some interesting negotiations between Torizo, a yakuza who wants the girl back, and Itto, who refuses to hand her over. The solution is typical of Itto; he agrees to undertake a series of tortures so that the girl can be set free, as described in a yakuza custom. It's a perfect opportunity to show just how tough Itto is; the entire time he is beaten, Itto doesn't make a sound, something which terrifies his torturers, and reinforces his stoic fortitude. Similarly, the supporting characters of *Baby Cart to Hades* add depth to the film, making it more than just an exercise in bloody action sequences. Kanbei, the conflicted ronin, and Genba, the treacherous and paranoid samurai, drive the more thought-provoking material in the film, providing an intriguing backdrop to the action.

The best aspect of *Baby Cart to Hades* is, of course, the epic battle scene, which takes place towards the end, in which Itto destroys Genba and his army singlehandedly. Despite the overblown manga style of the series, it must surely have been a challenge to choreograph such a scene convincingly. First Itto kills some enemies with guns and bombs, then he wades in, moving quickly among them, his blade flashing. Wakayama is at his bodycount best in these scenes, and moves with such fluidity and precision you simply enjoy the scene, never questioning its preposterous nature.

THE VERDICT

The *Lone Wolf and Cub* series was still going strong with its third film, featuring top-notch performances from Wakayama and Tomikawa, and plenty of the requisite, fiercely paced battle scenes.

Lady Snowblood (1972)

Japanese Title: *Shurayukihime*
Directed by: Toshiya Fujita
Written by: Adapted by Norio Osada from the manga by Kazuo Koike and Kazuo Kamimura
Produced by: Kikumaru Okuda

Edited by: Osamu Inoue
Cinematography: Masaki Tamura
Cast: Meiko Kaji (Yuki AKA Lady Snowblood), Toshio Kurosawa (Ryurei), Masaaki Daimon (Go), Miyoko Akaza (Sayo), Shinichi Uchida (Shiro), Takeo Chii (Tokuichi), Noburo Nakaya (Banzo), Yoshiko Nakada (Kobue), Akemi Negishi (Tajire), Kaoru Kusuda (Otora)

PLOT SUMMARY

Yuki Kashima is born into a life of vengeance. Her mother is unable to avenge the murders of her husband and child, so she conceives and gives birth to Yuki, in the hope that her daughter can finish what she started. Yuki is trained by a harsh samurai turned priest, and honed into a lethal assassin. Ready to begin her quest, Yuki employs the help of a clan of beggars to track down the gang of criminals who murdered her father and older brother 20 years earlier. First she finds Banzo, who has become a truly pathetic old man, reduced to cheating at gambling and living off the prostitution of his daughter, Kobue. He puts up no resistance as Yuki cuts him down. Yuki is disappointed to discover her next victim has seemingly already died, and angrily strikes at his tombstone. Yuki's mentor tells her story to a young journalist, Ryurei, in the hope that publicising her story will draw out Otora, the last survivor of the murderers. Yuki's attempts at revenge are frustrated yet again when, after a bloody exchange, Otora appears to hang herself. It turns out that Yuki's earlier target is not dead at all, and is in fact Ryurei's father, and a corrupt and wealthy weapons dealer. Yuki confronts and kills him, and Ryurei also dies in the process. Wounded, Yuki staggers into the snow, where she is stabbed by Kobue, intent on avenging her father.

ANALYSIS

Lady Snowblood is a compelling study of revenge, and a welcome counterpoint to the many genre films which glorify 'getting even'. The film also looks fantastic, with highly stylised direction from Toshiya Fujita.

Lady Snowblood is primarily concerned with showing the ultimate futility of revenge. This is illustrated through the experiences of Yuki, herself a living instrument of revenge. Yuki is a sympathetic protagonist rather than a heroic one; she has been trained to avenge the murders of her family her whole life, deprived of a normal existence and life's simple pleasures. The beautiful Meiko Kaji is perfectly cast in the role, convincingly portraying Yuki's pain as she is forced to make difficult decisions about her revenge and showing frightening rage when she confronts the real villain of the film.

The first victim of Yuki's revenge, Banzo, is a weak old man who offers no resistance to Yuki's blade. Hardly a satisfying victory. Worse still, she meets Kobue, his loving daughter, and must face the thought of depriving this girl of her father. Yuki's actions set Kobue on the same course she has been following; Kobue too must give up a normal life as she focuses on vengeance. *Lady Snowblood* thus reveals the futility of revenge; it is simply an endless cycle of violence which brings nothing but pain to all those involved.

True to the manga origins of *Lady Snowblood*, the story is told in a distinctive style. Director Fujita makes use of a number of interesting techniques. Yuki's murder of a gang leader at the film's beginning is extremely stylised; there is a slow-motion shot of Yuki as she somersaults over her opponents then a series of rapid shots as she dispatches them. There is no shortage of blood, and Fujita makes constant use of the red-on-white motif, either blood on snow or on the white portions of the Japanese flag. The montage in which a portion of novelist Ryurei's work on Yuki is read aloud is also very striking, and makes use of dynamic, manga-style art imposed over shots of people feverishly buying the book.

Interestingly, *Lady Snowblood* is listed as one of the inspirations for

Quentin Tarantino's *Kill Bill* films. Although both feature a tortured female protagonist seeking revenge, Tarantino takes the much more predictable route of glorifying revenge, rather than condemning it.

THE VERDICT

Lady Snowblood is a prime example of the samurai film's ability to interrogate notions of violence and revenge, and a must-see for fans of the genre.

Lone Wolf and Cub: Baby Cart in the Land of Demons (1973)

Japanese Title: *Kozure Okami: Meifumando*
Directed by: Kenji Misumi
Written by: Adapted by Kazuo Koike and Tsutomo Nakamura from the manga by Kazuo Koike and Goseki Kojima
Produced by: Masanori Sanada, Tomisaburo Wakayama
Edited by: Toshio Taniguchi
Cinematography: Fujio Morita
Cast: Tomisaburo Wakayama (Itto Ogami), Michiyo Yasuda (Shiranui), Akihiro Tomikawa (Daigoro), Shingo Yamashiro (Lord Naritaka), Tomomi Sato ('Quick Change' Oyoo), Satoshi Amatsu (Inspector Senzo), Minoru Ohki (Retsudo Yagyu)

PLOT SUMMARY

Itto is hired by Kuroda clan samurai, after they test his skill as a warrior. His assignment is to recover a document, which reveals that the young heir of the clan is in fact a girl, born to Naritaka (the current lord) and his favourite concubine. Naritaka's son, Matsumaru, the true heir, is being hidden in a tower. The document is in the possession of Jikei, a powerful Abbot, who intends to deliver it to the Yagyu, who will expose the scandal and ruin the clan. Finding Jikei at a temple, Itto finds he cannot bring himself to strike him, as Jikei has reached a state of perfect enlightenment. Meanwhile Daigoro has run into some trouble of his own. A pickpocket, 'Quick Change' Oyoo, leaves him holding her loot as she flees from Senzo, an inspector. Daigoro refuses to identify Oyoo, even when Senzo beats him. Oyoo is so touched by his loyalty she promises never to steal again. A Kuroda woman named Shiranui hires Itto to kill Naritaka, his mistress and the false heir, so that the true Matsumaru can become lord of the Kuroda, an assignment which Itto accepts. As Jikei sails across a river, Itto cuts the bottom of the boat out from under him, killing him swiftly underwater and taking the document. Shiranui intentionally wets the document, making it blank, but Ogami delivers it to the Kuroda anyway. In the castle of the Kuroda, Itto challenges Naritaka about his deception, and the lord orders his men to kill him. Itto defeats them, fighting his way to Naritaka and fulfilling his assignment. The young Lord Matsumaru is now able to take his rightful place.

ANALYSIS

Baby Cart in the Land of Demons is a return to form for the *Lone Wolf and Cub* series, after the slight disappointment of *Baby Cart in Peril*. This film is almost as good as *Baby Cart on the River Styx*, the best of the series.

Baby Cart in the Land of Demons is supported by a driving plot, which not only keeps the film moving at a nice pace, but also provides the excuse for compelling scenarios and visceral fight scenes. The idea that Itto must defeat a succession of samurai to begin his assignment, each one giving him a portion of his instructions and fee, is magnificent, and works very well on screen. Other plot elements, such as the Kuroda secret document which everyone wants and will kill to get, ensure that *Baby Cart in the Land of Demons* is always exciting in its twists and turns.

This film also contains some of the most violent and well-choreographed battle scenes in the *Lone Wolf and Cub* series. As usual, Tomisaburo Wakayama is magnificent. He moves with perfect precision in his fight scenes, and *Baby Cart in the Land of Demons* is full of classics. The duels towards the beginning, against the men sent to test him, are especially worthy of mention. The scenes of Itto fighting his way through the Kuroda palace are also particularly well realised, with plenty of rapid cuts and pans. The gore level is high; watch for the messenger giving Itto his assignment as he burns alive, or the brutal shot in which Itto literally cuts a man in half.

Also worthy of mention is the scene in which Daigoro stoically covers for a pickpocket, even when he's beaten by an inspector. Itto looks on, proud that his son has honourably kept his promise.

THE VERDICT

Director Kenji Misumi restores the *Lone Wolf and Cub* series to the former levels of excitement he reached with the second film in the series. Not only a welcome entry to the series, but a fine samurai film in its own right.

Lady Snowblood: Love Song of Vengeance (1974)

Japanese Title: *Shuri-yuki-hime: Urami Renga*
Directed by: Toshiya Fujita
Written by: Adapted by Kiyohide Ohara and Norio Osada from the manga by Kazuo Koike and Kazuo Kamimura
Produced by: Kikumaru Okuda
Edited by: Osamu Inoue
Cinematography: Tatsuo Suzuki
Cast: Meiko Kaji (Yuki AKA Lady Snowblood), Yoshio Harada (Shusuke), Kazuko Yoshiyuki (Aya), Shin Kishida (Kikui), Juzo Itami (Ransui)

PLOT SUMMARY

Yuki has survived the seemingly fatal wound she received at the end of the first film, but has been sentenced to death for her crimes. She is rescued by members of Japan's secret police, headed by Kikui, who wants Yuki to assassinate Ransui, an anarchist who poses a real threat to Kikui and Terauchi, the minister of justice. Yuki accepts the assignment and poses as Ransui's maid, but finds herself bonding with him and his wife, Aya. Ransui figures out that Yuki is Lady Snowblood, and explains to her that Kikui and Terauchi unlawfully executed a large group of his anarchist friends, and that he has a document which proves it. Should the document be made public, Kikui and Terauchi will be ruined. Yuki becomes Ransui's protector, but he is arrested. Yuki takes the document to Shusuke, Ransui's brother. Shusuke runs a clinic in a slum, but his motivations are different to his brother's. He plans to blackmail Kikui and Terauchi to give the people of the slums food and money. Ransui is beaten and tortured by the police, who eventually release him, but they have injected him with plague. He soon dies, and Aya, distraught with grief, attacks the police, who kill her. Shusuke reveals that Aya was once his wife, and left him for his brother. He continues with his blackmail plot, even though he too is now suffering from the plague. Yuki delivers Shusuke's terms to Kikui, who responds by setting fire to the slums, hoping to kill Shusuke and burn the document. Yuki finds Shusuke still alive among the wreckage, and together they attack Kikui and Terauchi, killing them. Shusuke himself dies in the fighting and Yuki is left alone again.

ANALYSIS

The second and final film of the Lady Snowblood series, *Love Song of Vengeance* is much more political than *Lady Snowblood*. Although the first had some political overtones, it was in the main a revenge-oriented tale. Rather than repeat this formula, the filmmakers chose to tell a very different and distinct story.

Unlike most samurai films, *Love Song of Vengeance* takes place in the Meiji era of Japanese history, just after the Russo-Japanese war of 1904–1905. This is after the abolition of the Shogunate and the dissolution of the samurai class, and the beginnings of a more industrialised

Japan. The political themes in the film focus around a pair of activist brothers and their struggle against some corrupt government officials. This makes for a compelling story, as Yuki, Ransui and Shusuke struggle against their powerful enemies, who go to great lengths to conceal their murderous pasts, even setting fire to a large slum, which is home to many people. The central theme of resistance against corrupt authority works very well in this film, reminiscent of the work of Masaki Kobayashi.

Despite its setting and preoccupations, the elements of the samurai film are still clearly present. Meiko Kaji as Yuki continues to slash her way through large groups of enemies, proving to be just as adept as other stars of the genre, such as Shintaro Katsu and Tomisaburo Wakayama. Toshiya Fujita continues his carefully styled direction, creating a variety of visually satisfying shots. Worthy of mention is the sequence towards the beginning of the film, where Yuki, cornered on a beach, surrenders herself to the police. Yuki throws her sword away, then there's a shot from above, as the police encircle Yuki, obscuring her from our view. Next we see a beautiful image of Yuki's sword, lodged in the ground, surrounded by the ocean, both the metal and water reflecting the sun and each other.

Unlike many sequels, *Love Song of Vengeance* allows Yuki's character to develop. It is disturbing to see her at the beginning of the film; she moves like a ghost, clearly tired of the fugitive's life she leads, and shows very little expression. For those who followed Yuki's painful journey in the first film, it is a pleasure to see her finally smile.

THE VERDICT

A very fitting sequel and a great film in its own right, *Love Song of Vengeance* builds on themes touched upon in *Lady Snowblood* as well as adding new elements. A standout example of the samurai film genre, not only because of its unusual heroine and setting, but also its superior quality.

Bandits vs. Samurai Squadron (1978)

Japanese Title: *Kumokiri Nizaemon*
Directed by: Hideo Gosha
Written by: Adapted by Kaneo Ikegami from the novel by Shotaro Ikenami
Produced by: Masahiro Sato, Ginichi Iwamoto, Shigemi Sugisaki
Edited by: Michio Suwa
Cinematography: Masao Kosugi
Cast: Tatsuya Nakadai (Nizaemon), Shima Iwashita (Ochiyo), Shogoro Ichikawa (Shikibu), Takashi Yamaguchi (Owari), Koshiro Matsumoto (Kuranosuke), Tetsuro Tamba (Kichibei), Keiko Matsuzaka (Oshino), Teruhiko Aoi (Rokunosuke), Mitsuko Baisho (Omatsu), Hiroyuki Nagato (Kichigoro)

PLOT SUMMARY

The Kumokiri, a gang of skilled thieves, continually avoid Shikibu, a samurai inspector.

Their latest plan is to rob the vault of a wealthy merchant, Matsuya. Nizaemon Kurokiri, the leader of the Kumokiri, sends Ochiyo, a seductive woman, to make Matsuya fall in love with her. Matsuya proposes to her, and Ochiyo, along with some of her accomplices, is able to infiltrate his household. Shikibu discovers that Nizaemon is really Iori Tsuji, a samurai whose brother was accused of embezzlement by the Owari clan. The Owari clan killed their family, while the two brothers were able to escape. Nizaemon's brother, Kuranosuke, urges him to seek revenge on the Owari by helping him kill their daimyo, but he refuses, no longer caring about their old life. Ochiyo discovers the location of Matsuya's vault and his keys, but Shikibu is waiting for them on the night of the heist. In a long brutal battle, only Nizaemon, Ochiyo and two other members of the gang escape. Kuranosuke gives himself up, pretending to be his brother. He is executed, along with the other captured members of the gang. When Nizaemon hears of his brother's sacrifice, he realises he must take his place in the assault on Lord Owari. Sneaking into the Owari castle, Nizaemon battles his way through Owari's retainers, but stops when he discovers that a child born to his ex-lover Oshino and heir to the Owari, is actually his, and not Lord Owari's. Nizaemon tries to escape with Oshino, but she is killed by their pursuers. Shikibu resigns his post, as he has discovered corruption in the Owari, and is sympathetic to the Tsuji brothers. When visiting Kuranosuke's grave, he and Nizaemon pass each other on the road.

ANALYSIS

Another film by Hideo Gosha, *Bandits vs. Samurai Squadron* combines elements from the two genres he was most familiar with: yakuza and samurai. The result is an epic tale of gangster heists and samurai-style revenge, a pleasing combination which benefits from Gosha's skilled direction.

Bandits vs. Samurai Squadron tells the story of the Kumokiri gang, a group which specialises in infiltrating the households of wealthy individuals, such as merchants and sake brewers, in order to rob them. The film's plot works very effectively to keep viewer attention; the devious ways in which the Kumokiri gang rob their targets, and the constant efforts of the valiant Inspector Shikibu to apprehend them, make for some entertaining scenes, in the tradition of classic heist films. The slowly unfolding plot gradually reveals the relationship between Nizaemon and Kuranosuke, and keeps the viewer wondering what this will mean for the two characters and the gang. There are also plenty of twists and changes in the plot, which keeps the story moving at a nice pace. The only criticism is that some of the twists come too late in the film, which means their implications do not have sufficient time to be explored.

At 2 hours 40 minutes, with a large cast of characters, and complex plot, there's always the potential for the viewer to become lost or confused. But the pace is perfect: not so slow that it becomes boring, and not so fast that we lose track of what's happening. Many of the characters assume false identities, and Gosha employs the simple technique of text on screen to show their name and true allegiance.

Gosha lends his distinctive sense of rhythm to the battle sequences. The fight between the samurai police and the Akatsuki gang at the beginning of the film is particularly good, complete with ingeniously paced squirts of blood that shoot out as the camera pans across the scene.

Tatsuya Nakadai as Nizaemon, is the strong, inexpressive boss of the Kumokiri gang, who loses everything, and then embarks on a selfless quest for revenge. As always, he excels at portraying both an inscrutable strength and a profound sense of loss. Shogoro Ichikawa is equally effective as Inspector Shikibu, lending credibility to this noble character who must change when he discovers corruption in the clan he works for. Also worthy of mention is Shima Iwashita, the beautiful yet harsh Ochiyo, master infiltrator of the Kumokiri gang.

THE VERDICT

A pleasing fusion of the yakuza and samurai genres, *Bandits vs. Samurai Squadron* is a solid film, although not quite as good as some of Gosha's earlier works. But like all his films, it's definitely worth seeing.

Hunter in the Dark (1979)

Japanese Title: *Yami no karyudo*
Directed by: Hideo Gosha
Written by: Adapted by Hideo Gosha from the novel by Shotaro Ikenami
Produced by: Masayuki Sato, Ginichi Kishimoto, Shigemi Sugisaki
Edited by: Michio Suwa
Cinematography: Tadashi Sakai
Cast: Tatsuya Nakadai (Gomyo), Yoshio Harada (Yataro), Sonny Chiba (Shimoguni), Ayumi Ishida (Oriwa), Keiko Kishi (Omon), Ai Kanzaki (Osaki), Kayo Matsuo (Oren), Tetsuro Tamba (Tanuma)

PLOT SUMMARY

Gomyo, a yakuza boss, hires Yataro, a ronin who has lost all memories of his past. He helps his new boss escape an attempt on his life by Omon, a woman jilted by Gomyo, and also manages to kill Jihei, Gomyo's rival. Omon escapes Gomyo's men, and is taken in by Kasuke, a poor fisherman. Meanwhile, Shimoguni, an ambitious samurai, is charged with the task of wiping out the Kitamae ronin, a group attempting to restore their clan. Shimoguni hires Gomyo to perform this task and sends Yataro after them. In a vicious battle he kills most of them, but a few escape. Recovering from his wounds in Gomyo's house, Yataro is recognised by Oriwa, who used to be his wife. Unable to bring his memory back, she sends him to a temple, where he will learn all the secrets of his past. Gomyo overhears all of this, and Shimoguni demands he hand over Yataro. At the temple, Yataro regains his memory; he is the last hope of the Kitamae clan, entrusted with a document proving the clan's ownership of the wealthy Ezo province. The remaining Kitamae ronin burst in and attack him, eager for revenge. In the confusion the temple catches fire, and Yataro is rescued both from the fire and his madness by Gomyo, who has him hidden in an old warehouse. Gomyo sends Oriwa to be with him, even though he loves her himself. Shimoguni destroys Gomyo's house, but discovers Yataro's whereabouts from Omon. Orei, a woman wanting to avenge Jihei, also finds Yataro, killing him in his weakened state, although he manages also to kill her. Shimoguni arrives in time to see Oriwa commit suicide, and leaves, confident he has been successful. Gomyo has recovered the Kitamae document, and confronts Shimoguni with it. In a final duel, the two kill each other.

ANALYSIS

Considered by many to be Hideo Gosha's best film of the 1970s, *Hunter in the Dark* is a gripping samurai film, combining Gosha's trademark direction with a compelling plot.

The film revolves around Yataro, a ronin with no memory whatsoever of his past. Throughout, small details about his identity are revealed, and the audience is left to piece them together. A number of other characters, each with their own bloody aims, most of which are closely intertwined with Yataro's past, ensure there's a constant sense of conflict and opposition in the film. Also, the character who actually ends up fulfilling the heroic role of *Hunter in the Dark* is very surprising, which lends great momentum to the later scenes.

The moment where Yataro finally regains his memory is hard to forget. Having just escaped a burning temple, weak from his wounds, Yataro cries out as he recalls the horrors of his past. With his clothes still smouldering, he swings his sword wildly, desperately attempting to kill the ghosts of his old life. Poetic moments are peppered throughout: when Yataro stares at a burning lantern, for instance, an image that plays an important part in his tragic past; or when Omon, a tough yakuza woman, kills Kasuke, one of her admirers, with the same hairpin which caused them to meet earlier in the film.

The battle scenes are of a very high standard. Yataro's battle with the Kitamae ronin is particularly impressive, and includes one of the most surprising severed arms ever shown in a samurai film. After defeating the ronin, Yataro is confronted by a group of vengeful yakuza women, who, in an intensely frenetic scene, almost succeed in killing him. The battle between Gomyo and Shimoguni is also realised with Gosha's usual skill, and takes place in the unique location of a large chicken coop. Tatsuya Nakadai and martial arts superstar Sonny Chiba bring a necessary energy to this scene, both swift and unpredictable.

Tatsuya Nakadai again demonstrates his considerable range in his performance as Gomyo, the tough yakuza boss who proves to be more than just a criminal. Yoshio Harada is also very engaging in his role, convincingly conveying anguish and pain when Yataro finally regains his memory. Keiko Kishi offers a frightening performance as Omon, a treacherous woman prepared to do anything to survive. Sonny Chiba is similarly well cast as the ruthlessly ambitious Shimoguni.

THE VERDICT

Yet another swiftly paced Gosha film, with a compelling plot and absorbing performances. A definite highlight of 1970s samurai films.

THE 1980s, 90s AND CURRENT CINEMA

By the 1980s, samurai films had lost much of their popularity, with audiences' attention turning instead to the yakuza (gangster) genre; and studios followed the money. Even Akira Kurosawa struggled to make his two samurai epics of the 1980s, *Kagemusha* and *Ran*, which were saved from cancellation by international funding. George Lucas and Francis Ford Coppola, both admirers of Kurosawa's films, provided him with the funds to finish *Kagemusha*, a haunting film telling the story of Takeda Shingen (a famous daimyo) and his body double.

Throughout the 1980s and 90s few samurai films were made, compared to the voluminous output of the 1960s. Recently, however, the samurai film has been enjoying somewhat of a revival. Popular directors in Japan are returning to the genre, creating films that are finding acclaim overseas. Yoji Yamada's trilogy of samurai films (*The Twilight Samurai*, *The Hidden Blade* and *Love and Honour*) were all popular among judges and audiences on the film festival circuit, and rightly so. Takeshi Kitano, a popular director of crime films, made his own version of *Zatoichi*, putting himself in the lead role, with great success: the film was not only popular with audiences, but also won a variety of awards both in Japan and abroad. The inflated style of the 1970s samurai films is still alive and well with films such as *Aragami*. Directed by Ryuhei Kitamura, famous for his flamboyant action films, *Aragami* is every bit as wonderfully overblown as the *Lone Wolf and Cub* series.

Kagemusha (1980)

Japanese Title: *Kagemusha*
Directed by: Akira Kurosawa
Written by: Masato Ide, Akira Kurosawa
Produced by: Akira Kurosawa, Tomoyuki Tanaka, Francis Ford Coppola (international release), George Lucas (international release)
Edited by: Yoshihiro Iwatani (assistant editor), Tome Minami (negative cutter)
Cinematography: Takao Saito, Shoji Ueda
Cast: Tatsuya Nakadai (Shingen Takeda/Shingen's double), Tsutomo Yamazaki (Nobukado Takeda), Kenichi Hagiwara (Katsuyori Takeda), Jinpachi Nezu (Sohachiro Tsuchiya), Hideji Otaki (Masakage Yamagata), Daisuke Ryu (Nobunaga Oda), Masayuki Yui (Ieyasu Tokugawa)

PLOT SUMMARY

A common thief is the exact likeness of Shingen Takeda, a powerful daimyo vying for control of Japan. The thief is trained as Shingen's double, so as to trick his enemies. When Shingen dies from a gunshot, the thief must take his place full time, so Shingen's enemies do not attempt to take advantage of his death. The thief is reluctant to accept this role, even trying to escape, but is moved by Shingen's secret funeral to change his mind. He grows bold in the role, becoming close to Shingen's grandson, Takemaru. Shingen's son, Katsuyori, becomes tired of pretending this thief is his father. Nobunaga and Ieyasu, rival daimyos, also try to gain control of Japan, first using spies and then an attack on Shingen's territory to discover whether or not he is still alive. But the double fools them, and they hold off on any further attacks. The illusion is shattered when the double attempts to ride Shingen's horse, which realises the thief isn't his master and throws him off. Exposed in front of a large crowd, the double is forced to leave. He finds himself unable to detach from the Takeda family, and watches Shingen's official funeral from behind a barrier with the other peasants. Katsuyori is now in charge of the Takeda, and he takes the army to attack Nobunaga. Nobunaga defeats the Takeda army with brilliant use of firearms. The double witnesses this and, heartbroken, charges Nobunaga's troops. He is shot, and dies lying in the water, the abandoned Takeda banner just out of his reach.

ANALYSIS

Kagemusha is another compelling film from master director Akira Kurosawa. Using real historical events as his inspiration, he crafts an emotive tale about the perils of adopting another's identity. What happens to someone who loses their own identity by assuming someone else's? This is the question Kurosawa explores.

Shingen's double finds he is unable to distance himself from the Takeda clan, even though he is no longer wanted by them. He has become so involved in Shingen's life that he cannot return to his own. Kurosawa predicts this through some interesting dialogue from Nobukado, Shingen's brother who also performed as his double on occasion, and with some skilful uses of cinematic techniques. Among the most memorable is when the double, dressed in Shingen's full armour, leaves a dimly lit room. His huge shadow looms menacingly above him, showing that he is only a shadow of the real Shingen and will suffer for letting another's identity obscure his own.

As usual, Kurosawa's direction creates many memorable images. In some battle scenes, the sky is lit a very dark red and the sight of the samurai commanders silhouetted atop a mountain reflects the bloody fighting going on below them. The film's final battle, in which Katsuyori completely ruins Shingen's army, contains a long sequence of the Takeda troops lying dead and wounded in the dirt, victims of Nobunaga's riflemen. Kurosawa never shies away from showing the true results of warfare, this time in vivid colour.

Tatusuya Nakadai gives a consummate performance as Shingen's double, switching seamlessly from playing a stern, forthright man, to the timid, more jovial figure. He shows us a man who has lost everything and is denied the one thing he has come to want. Nakadai's performance is unnerving in its conviction and his ability to elicit sympathy.

THE VERDICT

A rich, well-directed film that explores a fascinating theme. Highly recommended.

Ran (1985)

Japanese Title: *Ran*
Directed by: Akira Kurosawa
Written by: Adapted by Akira Kurosawa, Hideo Oguni and Masato Ide from William Shakespeare's *King Lear*
Produced by: Katsumi Furukawa, Masato Hara, Hisao Kurosawa, Serge Silberman
Edited by: Akira Kurosawa, Hideto Aga, Hajime Ishihara, Ryusuke Otsubo
Cinematography: Asakazu Nakai, Takao Saito, Masaharu Ueda
Cast: Tatsuya Nakadai (Hidetora), Akira Terao (Taro), Jinpachi Nezu (Jiro), Daisuke Ryu (Saburo), Mieko Harada (Kaede), Yoshiko Miyazaki (Sue), Hisashi Igawa (Kurogane), Peter (Kyoami), Masayuki Yui (Tango), Takeshi Nomura (Tsurumaru)

PLOT SUMMARY

Hidetora, a daimyo who has conquered a large area, wants to retire and announces his intention to abdicate to Taro, his eldest son. His other two sons, Jiro and Saburo, will get a castle each, and are expected to help their brother. Saburo sees the foolishness of this situation; he explains to his father that they will simply end up fighting each other, but Hidetora banishes him for his troubles. Fujimaki, another daimyo, is impressed with Saburo's honesty and courage and asks him to marry his daughter, an offer which he accepts. Taro's wife, Kaede, convinces him to assert more authority over Hidetora; this angers Hidetora and he leaves to stay with Jiro, who turns him away on orders from Taro. With nowhere to go, Hidetora and his escort capture a castle held by one of Taro's generals. Betrayed by two of his samurai, Hidetora is attacked by his two sons and flees into a storm, where he finally succumbs to madness. Jiro has Taro killed, and becomes the new daimyo. Hidetora is found by Tango and Kyoami, his fool, but he has suffered a complete emotional breakdown. Saburo hears of his father's plight, and arrives with a small force, making it clear that he only wants to take Hidetora away with him. Saburo finds his father and they share a painful reunion. Hidetora finally emerges from his madness, and is content. Jiro betrays Saburo, sending riflemen, who kill him. Upon seeing this, Hidetora dies from grief. Jiro finds himself trapped in his castle, surrounded by rival daimyos, who take advantage of his weakness.

ANALYSIS

In many ways, *Ran* is a dream come true for fans of samurai films: the most influential director of the genre, Akira Kurosawa, bringing to the screen an epic saga, on a Hollywood-scale budget.

Ran is a big film. It features big performances from a superb cast, large battles, extensive sets and an epic plot. It is difficult not to get caught up in its grand scale. There are scenes that involve hundreds of extras, all dressed for battle; a castle, built specially for the film, is burned to the ground; and Kurosawa makes use of grand locations, such as the beautiful mountainous terrain at the film's beginning and the huge empty plain at its end. Such scale comes at a price and it's easy to see why Kurosawa ran into trouble finishing this film. Fortunately, he persevered. The tone and imagery of *Ran* is luxurious, a feast for the senses.

Nonetheless, for those familiar with Kurosawa's earlier work, *Ran* seems to lack a little of the simplistic brilliance which characterises films such as *Seven Samurai*, *Yojimbo* and *Throne of Blood*.

It is hard to think of any scenes in *Ran* that are as purely entertaining and evocative as the opening scene of *Throne of Blood* but Kurosawa does create some wonderful images: the billowing clouds forming over Hidetora as he makes his fateful decision to abdicate in favour of his sons foreshadow the storm that will come when they betray him; the battle for the castle, accompanied by sombre music, playing over the shots of carnage; Tsurumaru, the blind man, standing completely alone in the battlements of his ruined castle, waiting for his sister, who will never come. Lacking something of the poetry of Kurosawa's earlier work, such images are beautifully composed, presented in vibrant, arresting colours.

An adaptation of Shakespeare's *King Lear*, Kurosawa uses this rich material to its full potential. *Ran* is a compelling examination of a man, Hidetora, who, through his own folly, loses everything he has gained throughout his life. As in *Kagemusha*, Tatsuya Nakadai plays a man descending into madness. Particularly memorable is the scene in which Hidetora, having lost a battle against his two treacherous sons and cornered in a burning castle, walks quietly down the castle stairs, an unchanging look of shock on his face. Fires rage around him, and he is surrounded by his enemies, but Hidetora walks quietly down the stairs and out the gates. Nakadai performs what must have been a difficult scene with complete conviction, and the result is unforgettable. Mieko Harada also offers an unnerving performance as Kaede, a woman seething with hatred. The single-named Peter does very well as Kyoami, Hidetora's fool, who cannot help but love his master, despite his decisions.

THE VERDICT

Although lacking some of the poetry of Kurosawa's earlier films, *Ran* is still a worthy entry to the genre, with a rich plot and some captivating performances. But if you haven't seen any of Kurosawa's samurai films, you might do better to start with his earlier work.

The Twilight Samurai (2002)

Japanese Title: *Tasogare Seibei*
Directed by: Yoji Yamada
Written by: Adapted by Yoji Yamada and Yoshitaka Asama from the novels by Shuuhei Fujisawa
Produced by: Hiroshi Fukazawa, Shigehiro Nakagawa, Ichiro Yamamoto
Edited by: Iwao Ishii
Cinematography: Mutsuo Naganuma
Cast: Hiroyuki Sanada (Seibei), Rie Miyazawa (Tomoe), Nenji Kobayashi (Choubei), Ren Osugi (Toyotarou), Mitsuru Fukikoshi (Michinojo), Hiroshi Kanbe (Naota), Min Tanaka (Zenemon), Tetsuro Tamba (Tozaemon)

PLOT SUMMARY

Seibei Iguchi is a poor samurai, forced to care for his two daughters and senile old mother alone after his wife dies. Without the proper money for bathing and grooming, Seibei is criticised by his fellow samurai, and given the nickname 'Twilight' because he has to hurry home each evening to look after his children. After helping his childhood friend Tomoe escape her abusive husband, the two grow close, but Seibei decides not to marry her because he fears she won't like his frugal lifestyle. Political turmoil wracks Japan, and many in Seibei's clan are ordered to commit suicide as the power balance shifts. One such samurai, Zenemon, refuses to do so, and Seibei is ordered to kill him. About to carry out his mission, Seibei realises that he wants Tomoe as his wife, but she tells him she has accepted another proposal. After a bloody duel, Seibei kills Zenemon, and finds Tomoe waiting for him. The two wed, but Seibei dies in a war three years later. Seibei is remembered fondly by his youngest daughter, who knows he lived a full, albeit short, life.

ANALYSIS

The Twilight Samurai is a standout samurai film and proof that the genre is alive and well in modern cinema. The film is a simple story told beautifully. *The Twilight Samurai* centres around Seibei, a samurai, and his family, and despite the fact that they're desperately poor and barely surviving, the scenes of them all together create a warm atmosphere. The scenes' strength comes from the convincing relationship between Seibei and his daughters, and director Yoji Yamada works hard to emphasise their closeness, showing the family in a variety of simple, day-to-day moments. Seibei appears to be a man before his times; he is a caring single father, encouraging his daughters to learn to read and treating them with kindness and good humour, despite the understandable stress of his domestic situation.

The love story that plays out between Seibei and Tomoe is subtle and touching rather than melodramatic and clichéd, conveying true affection with very little dialogue, through glances and expressions.

The Twilight Samurai presents one of the most realistic visions of samurai life in the Tokugawa era. Yamada's preoccupation with the routine life of the samurai adds a level of realism to his film, as we see characters engaged in rather unremarkable activities. Seibei works with several other samurai as a public servant in the food stores of his clan's castle, keeping track of the supplies. Shots of samurai working at their desks, rather than at war, show the administrative duties that were a large part of most samurai's lives in the Tokugawa era. Yet when Yamada is required to show violence he does so with startling realism, and Seibei's battle with the insane Zenemon has to be one of the most convincing in any samurai film. The two flail wildly at each other with their blades, beginning to slow down and limp as wounds and exhaustion take their toll. This plays in stark contrast to the assured duels of so many samurai films, which are over in a few swift strikes.

This marriage of realism and in-depth characterisation is the greatest triumph of Yamada's film.

THE VERDICT

The Twilight Samurai is a touching story bolstered by impressive realism and rounded characterisation. Essential viewing.

Zatoichi (2003)

Japanese Title: *Zatoichi*
Directed by: Takeshi Kitano
Written by: Adapted by Takeshi Kitano from a story by Kan Shimozawa
Produced by: Masayuki Mori, Tsunehisa Saito
Edited by: Takeshi Kitano, Yoshinori Oota
Cinematography: Katsumi Yanagishima
Cast: Takeshi Kitano (Zatoichi), Tadanobu Asano (Hattori), Michiyo Ookusu (Oume), Daigoro Tachibana (Seitaro/Osei), Yuuko Daike (Okinu), Yui Natsukawa (O-Shino), Ittoku Kishibe (Ginzo), Saburo Ishikura (Ogi), Akira Emoto (Torakichi), Ben Hiura ('Gramps')

PLOT SUMMARY

Zatoichi, the blind swordsman, arrives at a small town, where residents are troubled by the powerful alliance of two yakuza bosses, Ginzo and Ogi. Zatoichi stays with Oume, a woman who manages a small farm on her own. A ronin named Hattori arrives in town. His wife is ill, and he needs money to treat her, so he takes a job as a yojimbo (bodyguard) for Ginzo. Zatoichi and Shinkichi meet two geishas, Okinu and Osei (actually a man), who have been seeking the men who murdered their parents ten years ago. When Ginzo's yakuza attempt to cheat him at gambling, Zatoichi attacks them, killing many. Hattori arrives to stop him, but is too late. Meanwhile Okinu and Osei discover that Ogi was one of the men responsible for the murder of their family. A strange figure gives orders to Ginzo and Ogi, telling them he suspects he knows the truth about the two geishas. When the tavern owner discovers where Zatoichi and the geishas are staying, he sends some men, who burn down Oume's house. Ginzo and Ogi attempt to trap Okinu and Osei, but Zatoichi saves them, killing Ogi in the process. Following Ginzo to the beach, Zatoichi finds Hattori and defeats him in a tense duel. Ginzo flees and is found the next morning drowned in the river. Zatoichi finds the real bosses, Tarakichi the tavern owner, and his waiter, 'Gramps'. Zatoichi kills Tarakichi and blinds 'Gramps', who was Ginzo and Ogi's boss all along, as punishment for his crimes. With their town finally free of criminals, Oume and the other townsfolk enjoy the festival.

ANALYSIS

Zatoichi is back, and you've never seen him like this before. Director Takeshi Kitano, famous for his popular Japanese crime films, tried his hand at the character in 2003, and created a refreshingly different film, clearly distinct from the original series.

Kitano's Zatoichi is very different to the series produced throughout the 1960s, 70s and 80s, which may prove unsettling to fans of those films. Kitano, who not only directs but also stars as the blind swordsman, presents a Zatoichi that is in many ways the opposite of Shintaro Katsu's. Zatoichi has very few lines in this film, and often communicates with grunts and mumbled words, a far cry from Katsu's very vocal hero.

Katsu's Zatoichi was a product of his unique talent, and anyone trying to imitate his performance would only end up the victim of unfavourable comparisons. Kitano's Zatoichi makes a very interesting hero; he's utterly inscrutable, which leaves the audience constantly wondering what his plans are.

There is a very amusing thread of comedy running through *Zatoichi*. Shinkichi, a clumsy gambler, features in some highly comedic scenes, in particular when he tries to teach some farmers how to wield a sword, and then attempts to master Zatoichi's gambling technique.

Kitano uses rhythm very effectively in *Zatoichi*: the sounds of farmers working in a field, carpenters building a house and rain drops falling into a bucket create catchy tunes which synthesise with the images they accompany. The extended festival dance towards the end of the film is bizarre and unexpected, but visually lush and thrilling.

Zatoichi contains a great deal of graphic violence, even for a samurai film. Hattori, Zatoichi's strongest enemy in the film, is a highly effective ronin character, as sinister as he is skilled, and both he and the blind swordsman feature in some highly creative fight sequences. Kitano uses digital effects to take the violence to a new level, showing severed body parts and blood sprays with more realism than ever before. The fight scenes are well executed; Kitano clearly has a talent for frenetic, visceral battles. Particularly worthy of mention is the scene where Hattori hacks his way through the entire Funamachi gang, and the scene where Zatoichi fights a large group of yakuza in the heavy rain. Thanks to Kitano's modern style of directing and use of digital effects, all the battles in *Zatoichi* are extremely slick.

THE VERDICT

Rather than follow the pattern established by Shintaro Katsu, Takeshi Kitano creates his own version of the Zatoichi character, different yet no less entertaining. Taking a fresh approach, Kitano's *Zatoichi* shows that the samurai film genre is still ripe for exploitation in the current cinema landscape.

Aragami (2003)

Japanese Title: *Aragami*
Directed by: Ryuhei Kitamura
Written by: Ryuhei Kitamura, Ryuichi Takatsu

Produced by: Yuuji Ishida, Shinya Kawai, Haruo Umekawa
Edited by: Shuichi Kakesu
Cinematography: Takumi Furuya
Cast: Takao Osawa (the samurai), Masaya Kato (the master of the temple), Kanae Uotani (the woman of the temple), Tak Sakaguchi (new challenger), Hideo Sakai (the samurai's friend)

PLOT SUMMARY

Two wounded samurai fleeing a battle arrive at an old temple in the mountains, where they both collapse in exhaustion. One of the samurai awakens and begins to talk to the master of the temple, a strange man who has travelled far and wide, collecting a variety of objects from around the world. A woman sits and watches them talk, never speaking herself. Through conversation, the samurai discovers he was fed the specially prepared liver of his companion, which is why he was able to survive his fatal wounds. Enraged, he attacks his host, who stabs him through the chest. The samurai isn't even wounded; as the temple master explains, only a sword through his heart or head can kill him now. The temple master goes on to explain that he is in fact Miyamoto Musashi, and has never been defeated in battle. He is a near immortal super human, and can only be killed in the same way as the samurai. Musashi is tired of living, and wants to die in a duel. The samurai agrees to fight him, and chooses an unusual sword. In the battle that follows, the samurai seems to lose, but discovers a hidden power within himself. The samurai is victorious, and Musashi can finally rest and dream as he has been craving. The samurai discovers that the woman is Aragami, a goddess of war, and he agrees to stay with her in the temple, continuing to fight challengers just as Musashi did.

ANALYSIS

Aragami is another fine example of a recent samurai film, the work of action/horror director Ryuehi Kitamura. Kitamura is famous for fast-paced and stylistic fight scenes, and *Aragami* is no exception, featuring beautiful battles that are a feast for the senses.

The overall style of *Aragami* is even more overblown than that of the manga-inspired samurai films of the 1970s, such as the *Lone Wolf and Cub* series. *Aragami* seems to have a lot in common with the loud, over-the-top style of Japanese anime and video games, and this is especially true in the highly stylised fight sequences. Kitamura has a good under-standing of tone, and uses it to craft some highly atmospheric moments. While action is the main focus of *Aragami*, Kitamura and co-writer Ryuichi Takatsu create an intriguing, though not overly complex, plot.

Taking place entirely in the confines of a creepy temple, *Aragami* gradually builds to a climactic duel between the film's two main charac-ters. These scenes are composed mainly of the samurai and his host talking, and slowly reveal the disturbing situation the samurai finds himself in. Despite its simple structure, the viewer's interest is constantly piqued by mysteries and revelations.

Kitamura creates an unsettling atmosphere; inside the temple are rusty chains, weathered rafters and a large, solemn, stone statue (whose expression changes throughout the film), all lit to cast long shadows. The setting matches some of the more horrific revelations in the film, and creates the right level of menace when the fierce battle rages at the conclusion.

The battles present some of the most stylised violence ever shown in a samurai film. The scene where the samurai and his host fight in complete darkness, with only the sparks coming off their swords for illu-mination, is utterly stunning. The thrash rock soundtrack by Nobuhiko Morino exhilarates, complementing the modern anime feel of the film.

THE VERDICT

An atmospheric film with an intriguing plot and a grand duel at its conclusion, *Aragami* is a worthy addition to the samurai film genre. While Yoji Yamada continues the work of the more reflective filmmakers, such as Kurosawa, we can rest assured the action-oriented samurai film is still alive and well in *Aragami*.

The Hidden Blade (2004)

Japanese Title: *Kakushi ken oni no tsume*
Written by: Adapted by Yoshitaka Asama and Yoji Yamada from the novel by Shuuhei Fujisawa
Directed by: Yoji Yamada
Produced by: Hiroshi Fukazawa
Edited by: Iwao Ishii
Cinematography: Mutsuo Naganuma
Cast: Masatoshi Nagase (Munezo), Takako Matsu (Kie), Yukiyoshi Ozawa (Yaichiro), Hidetaka Yoshioka (Samon), Min Tanaka (Kansai Toda), Tomoko Tabata (Shino), Ken Ogata (Hori), Nenji Kobayashi (Ogata), Reiko Takashima (Yaichiro's wife)

PLOT SUMMARY

Munezo is a samurai of the Unesaka clan, learning to use new European rifles and artillery. Kie, a peasant girl who used to work at Munezo's house, has married into the Iseya family, who badly mistreat her. Weak from disease and exhaustion, Kie nearly dies, but Munezo takes her away from the Iseya, saving her life with medical treatment from a doctor. Meanwhile, Munezo's friend, Yoichiro, has been found guilty of ploting against the Shogun in Edo. He is brought back to the Unesaka lands where he is held prisoner. Untrue rumours begin to spread that Kie is Munezo's mistress, and when she is recovered, despite loving her, Munezo sends her back to her father. Yoichiro escapes from his prison and holds a peasant family hostage. Hori, the senior retainer of the clan, orders Munezo to kill him. Munezo visits his old teacher, Toda, who teaches him a new technique to defeat Yoichiro, who is considered one of the finest swordsmen in the Unesaka clan. Yoichiro's wife attempts to convince Munezo to spare him, even offering to sleep with him, but Munezo refuses. She also visits Hori. Munezo and Yoichiro fight, and Munezo wins, but is disappointed to see Yoichiro gunned down by Unesaka riflemen. He discovers that Hori slept with Yoichiro's wife, promising to spare Yoichiro, a promise he never had any intention of keeping. Enraged, Munezo uses his hidden blade technique to kill Hori, hoping this will allow Yoichiro and his wife, who has committed suicide, to rest in peace. Munezo renounces his samurai status to become a merchant, and marries Kie.

ANALYSIS

Along with *The Twilight Samurai*, *The Hidden Blade* cements Yoji Yamada's reputation as one of the finest directors of samurai films working in the current cinema landscape. Both films skilfully combine touching and humorous moments with moving personal drama and conflict.

There are certain thematic similarities between this film and *The Twilight Samurai*. Both feature a main character whose compassion alienates him from his peers, who is forced by his superiors to kill a man he respects and admires. However, *The Hidden Blade* is clearly distinct from Yamada's previous film, and is not simply a re-working of previous thematic content. Unlike Seibei in *The Twilight Samurai*, Munezo, the protagonist in *The Hidden Blade*, has the respect of his peers, and actually makes an effort to keep it, causing considerable dramatic tension. The film begins with Munezo saving Kie, a young peasant girl who used to be a servant at his mother's house, from the cruel merchant family she has married into. People begin to gossip that she is Munezo's mistress, and although he loves her, he sends her away, for the sake of both their reputations. Seibei, by comparison, puts the happiness of his loved ones before his reputation. *The Hidden Blade* also has added drama in Munezo's struggle against Hori, his corrupt superior. Hori is a cruel man, and makes an interesting counterpoint to Munezo's compassion. Unseen for much of the film, he drives the plot, his corruption forcing Munezo and Yoichiro into conflict, and ultimately leading Munezo in a completely new direction.

Like *The Twilight Samurai* the major strength of this film is Yamada's grasp of characterisation. Through a series of candid domestic scenes, he brings us into the midst of Munezo and Kie's lives, and this closeness adds weight to later scenes. We cannot help but feel empathy with these characters, something helped greatly by the strong performances of Masatoshi Nagase and Takako Matsu. As in Yamada's earlier work, there's a warm feeling in aspects of the film, generated mainly by the tender family moments shared by the characters.

One of the most interesting aspects of *The Hidden Blade* is its exploration of the modernisation of the samurai armies. Munezo's clan, the Unesaka, are in the process of training their men in the use of modern European rifles and artillery. Rather than take the predictable route and show these weapons in action on the battlefield, Yamada shows us the problems encountered by the samurai as they learn how to use them. Humorous scenes have the instructor from Edo, wearing his European suit, collar and neck-tie, growing increasingly frustrated with the Unesaka samurai, who do not understand the relevance of European traditions such as drills and synchronised marching. Yamada does briefly show the devastating effects of the new cartridge-loading rifles – they completely destroy a human arm in one scene – but for the most part uses much more subtle means to convey the effects of modern weapons on the samurai traditions. This theme is handled much more intelligently and effectively than in the rather obvious ending of Hollywood's attempt at the samurai film, *The Last Samurai*.

THE VERDICT

Another great film by Yamada, born from his firm grasp of characterisation, realism and compelling material.

Love and Honour (2006)

Japanese Title: *Bushi no ichibun*
Directed by: Yoji Yamada
Written by: Adapted by Yoji Yamada, Emiko Hiramatsu and Ichiro Yamamoto from the novel by Shuuhei Fujisawa.
Produced by: Hiroshi Fukazawa, Ichiro Yamamoto
Edited by: Iwao Ishii
Cinematography: Mutsuo Naganuma
Cast: Takuya Kimura (Shinnojo Mimura), Rei Dan (Kayo Mimura), Mitsugoro Bando (Toya Shimada), Takashi Sasano (Tokuhei), Kaori Momoi (Ine Hatano), Nenji Kobayashi (Sakunasuke Higuchi), Ken Ogata (Shinnojo's teacher)

PLOT SUMMARY

Shinnojo works as a food taster for his daimyo, ensuring that none of his meals are poisoned. Not enjoying this boring work, he hopes to one day open his own fencing school. While performing his duty, Shinnojo eats shellfish that wasn't prepared properly, making it toxic. He prevents his daimyo from eating the same food but grows ill from its effects and loses his sight completely. His loving wife, Kayo, does her best to care for him, but Shinnojo becomes increasingly depressed. His family insist that Kayo visit Shimada, a high-ranking samurai she knows, to ask him to make sure that they'll continue to be supported by the clan. This seems to work, and Shinnojo is happy for a time, no longer needing to worry about his livelihood. But he begins to suspect Kayo of having an affair and sends his servant, Tokuhei, to follow her. Kayo has been sleeping with Shimada, in exchange for his help. When Shinnojo discovers this, he divorces Kayo. He later realises Shimada tricked her; he actually had nothing to do with the daimyo's decision to continue supporting Shinnojo. He is enraged, and determines to kill Shimada. Adapting his swordsmanship to his blindness, Shinnojo challenges Shimada, and defeats him. Tokuhei brings Kayo back to him, and Shinnojo realises he treated her badly, but she still loves him.

ANALYSIS

Love and Honour is the third in Yoji Yamada's recent trilogy of samurai films, and, like the two previous entries, benefits from his expert use of characterisation and exceptional attention to detail.

Like *The Twilight Samurai* and *The Hidden Blade*, *Love and Honour* focuses on one samurai, learning an important lesson through adversity. In many ways Shinnojo is reminiscent of Seibei and Munezo; he has Seibei's modern attitudes to education (he plans to start a fencing school catering to people of all classes) and Munezo's firm sense of samurai pride. Shinnojo, however, is far less attuned to the feelings of others around him than Yamada's previous heroes, and this, in many ways, is the flaw he must overcome in the film. The Shinnojo we meet at the beginning of the film shows a lack of appreciation of those who care for him; he mocks both his loving wife Kayo and his loyal old servant, Tokuhei, failing to understand that these are the two most important people in his life. This makes Shinnojo considerably more flawed than both Seibei and Munezo, and thus his journey is a much harder one.

The simple plot of *Love and Honour* is both captivating and moving; only the hardest of audiences would fail to be moved by Shinnojo's painful journey. When he loses his sight, he loses his reason to live; he believes he can no longer function as an effective member of society, and this is a huge blow to his pride. We watch Shinnojo give in to anger and then despair, before he is finally able to find a purpose in his life again. Also touching is the plight of Kayo, who makes huge sacrifices to help her husband, but only suffers herself as a result, as a distraught Shinnojo badly mistreats her. The counterpoint to both Shinnojo and Kayo is Toya Shimada, an evil man whose actions drive the plot forward to its violent climax.

This moving plot is greatly assisted by performances from a well-chosen cast. Takuya Kimura is utterly convincing in his role, and flawlessly ranges the gamut of emotions that Shinnojo goes through during his painful journey. Rei Dan is charming as Kayo, presenting a touching impression of a woman who cares deeply for her husband. The two share some beautiful scenes together, for example when Kayo lovingly nurses Shinnojo out of a fever. Takashi Sasano puts in a fine performance as Tokuhei, who functions as a source of gentle comedy throughout the film. Sasano perfectly captures the humorous aspects of Tokuhei's character, when he practises fencing with a samurai child for instance, and skilfully conveys his dedication to Shinnojo and Kayo.

As in his other samurai films, Yamada creates an extremely realistic impression of Tokugawa-era Japan, showing us the daily routines of his characters. Shinnojo's job as a food taster for his daimyo, a seemingly exciting role, is portrayed instead as a mundane job; the food tasters sit in a row, eat a single mouthful of a dish, and then the food is rushed away to the daimyo's luxurious chambers. The domestic scenes involving Kayo and Tokuhei are similarly realistic, not only giving an interesting insight into times past, but also helping us to grow closer to Yamada's characters.

The duel between Shinnojo and Shimada is particularly well handled. Yamada treats the idea of a blind swordsman more practically than the Zatoichi films; Shinnojo's movements are entirely consistent with someone who has lost his sight; each time he attempts to strike his opponent he swings his sword multiple times, hoping to reach his mark. The duel's conclusion is sudden and surprising.

THE VERDICT

Another strong film from Yamada, who should be applauded for making samurai films of such a consistently high quality. The genre will survive long into the future if more films of this calibre are made.

BIBLIOGRAPHY

Galloway, Patrick, *Stray Dogs and Lone Wolves: The Samurai Film Handbook*, Berkeley: Stone Bridge Press, 2005.

Kure, Mitsuo, *Samurai: An Illustrated History*, Massachusetts: Tuttle Publishing, 2002.

Ratti, Oscar and Westbrook, Adele, *Secrets of the Samurai: The Martial Arts of Feudal Japan*, Massachusetts: Tuttle Publishing, 1973.

Silver, Alain, *The Samurai Film*, Woodstock: The Overlook Press, Peter Mayer Publishers, Inc., 2005.

Wilson, William Scott, *The Lone Samurai: The Life of Miyamoto Musashi*, Tokyo: Kodansha International, 2004.

Yoshimoto, Mitsuhiro, *Kurosawa: Film Studies and Japanese Cinema*, North Carolina: Duke University Press, 2000.

INDEX

kamera BOOKS

ESSENTIAL READING FOR ANYONE INTERESTED IN FILM AND POPULAR CULTURE

Tackling a wide range of subjects from prominent directors, popular genres and current trends through to cult films, national cinemas and film concepts and theories. Kamera Books come complete with complementary DVDs packed with additional material, including feature films, shorts, documentaries and interviews.

Silent Cinema
Brian J. Robb

A handy guide to the art of cinema's silent years in Hollywood and across the globe.

978-1-904048-63-3 **£9.99**

Dalí, Surrealism and Cinema
Elliott H. King

This book surveys the full range of Dalí's eccentric activities with(in) the cinema.

978-1-904048-90-9 **£9.99**

East Asian Cinema
David Carter

An ideal reference work on all the major directors, with details of their films.

978-1-904048-68-8 **£9.99**

David Lynch
Colin Odell & Michelle Le Blanc

Examines Lynch's entire works, considering the themes, motifs and stories behind his incredible films.

978-1-84243-225-9 **£9.99**